PANCHAYATI RAJ IN SCHEDULED AREAS

About the Author

Dr. P.S.K. Menon, having about 35 years of experience in Tribal Development has contributed immensely to the literature on tribal development and gender issues. He held official positions in different capacities in the Tribal and Harijan Welfare Department of Government of Madhya Pradesh, in the Government of India in the Ministries of Home Affairs and Welfare and in the Planning Commission and the National Commission for Women.

Prof. Bakshi D. Sinha, Economist has five decades of experience in research in social sciences. He has served as Professor in Universities in India and abroad and also as head of the research organizations such as Ford Foundation, NCERT and Birla Institute. He was educated in Bihar and Holland. Prof. Sinha has done considerable work on urban, rural and SC/STs problems apart from micro and macro planning. He has several publications to his credit.

PANCHAYATI RAJ IN SCHEDULED AREAS

A Critical Study

P.S.K. MENON

BAKSHI D. SINHA

Published for

INSTITUTE OF SOCIAL SCIENCES
NEW DELHI

by

CONCEPT PUBLISHING COMPANY, NEW DELHI-110059

ISBN 81-8069-027-X

First Published 2003

Published and Printed by
Ashok Kumar Mittal
Concept Publishing Company
A/15-16, Commercial Block, Mohan Garden
New Delhi-110059 (India)
Phones: 25351460, 25351794
Fax: 091–(11)–25357103
E-mail: publishing@conceptpub.com

Foreword

The tribal societies were accustomed to regulation of their domestic, religious, social, economic, socio-political and judicial affairs at the grass-roots level through their traditional tribal councils and collective wisdom of the people in the villages. Although, the Seventy-third Constitution Amendment Act, 1992, incorporated many important provisions with regard to Panchayats, yet, it restricted the application of Part IX provisions to the Scheduled and Tribal Areas under Article 243 (M). Subsequently, Mr. D.S. Bhuria, M.P. was appointed as Chairman of the Committee to recommend modifications in the Amendment Act that are needed for its application to the Scheduled and Tribal Areas. The Committee submitted its Report in January 1995 and thereafter, the Panchayats (Extension to the Scheduled Areas) Act, 1996, was enacted on 24 December 1996.

The Institute of Social Sciences, New Delhi extends its deep sense of gratitude to the Ministry of Tribal Affairs, Government of India for sponsoring the project on "Panchayati Raj in Scheduled Areas: A Critical Study", a subject so dear to the Institute. We intend pursuing vigorously the crucial issues raised in the Study Report to translate into action the provisions of the Extension Act, particularly that of working of Gram Sabha in the Scheduled Areas.

I would like to place on record our appreciation to the Study Team headed by Dr. P.S.K. Menon and ably assisted by Prof. Bakshi D. Sinha from its inception. Both worked with dedication to focus on essential areas requiring attention. Dr. Mahi Pal, a specialist in this field was an honorary consultant to this project.

We trust that the Ministry of Tribal Affairs would find this Study Report useful for accelerating the pace of participatory democracy in the Scheduled Areas.

October, 2000

GEORGE MATHEW
Director

Preface

The Working Group Report (May, 1996) on the Ninth Five Year Plan (1997-2002) made the significant observation that the "Tribals continue to form the poorest, most backward and most vulnerable section of Indian society despite all developmental strategies, programmes and schemes including Tribal Sub-Plan strategy .....As globalisation and liberalisation usher in fierce economic competition, only the fittest can survive and the weakest, particularly the tribals, may be driven to the wall unless protective measures are taken for safeguarding the tribals from the onslaught and urgent steps are taken to develop their skill and competitive ability".

The apt observation and recommendations of the said Working Group, and earlier to it, that of the High Level Expert Committee constituted by the Government of India under the Chairmanship of Shri Dileep Singh Bhuria, Member of Parliament, in June, 1994, to make recommendations on the salient features of the law for extending the provisions of the Constitution (73rd Amendment) Act, 1992, to the Scheduled Areas and subsequent enactment of the Panchayats (Extension of the Scheduled Areas) Act, 1996, with effect from 24 December, 1996, are some of the important measures adopted to establish grass-roots democracy in the Scheduled Areas in accordance with the ethos of the local tribal people and spirit of Constitutional provisions.

The formation of the Ministry of Social Justice and Empowerment, a couple of years ago, and the establishment of a separate Ministry of Tribal Affairs in October 1999 under the charge of a Scheduled Tribe Minister are signs of greater awareness among the national leadership to tackle the problems afflicting Tribal areas with a sense of urgency and understanding to yield tangible results for betterment of the tribal people.

The present project on "Panchayati Raj in Scheduled Areas: A Critical Study" entrusted to the Institute of Social Sciences, New Delhi, was undertaken from May, 1999 for a period of ten months with the following specific objectives:

1. to examine whether the Panchayats in the Scheduled Areas in the States of Andhra Pradesh, Bihar, Gujarat, Himachal Pradesh, Madhya Pradesh, Maharashtra, Orissa and Rajasthan have been endowed with such powers and authority as may be necessary to enable them to function as institutions of self-government, as envisaged in the 1996 Act, with critical analysis;
2. to study the nature, functions and the role of Gram Sabha to discharge functions specified in the 1996 Act;
3. to suggest measures to achieve the goals, envisaged in extending the provisions of Part IX of the Constitution; and
4. to study all other related issues *vis-à-vis,* Tribal Sub-Plan mechanism, administration, etc. in relation to Panchayati Raj in Scheduled Areas and make recommendations.

In order to achieve the above objectives, we made critical evaluation and comparative analysis of the implementation of the provisions of the Extension Act, 1996 and Conformity State Panchayat Acts, with special reference to the Powers of Gram Sabha. It was based on field studies in the States of Maharashtra and Orissa; and some of the Panchayats in Rajasthan. The anguish and helplessness in realising that at the grass-roots level matters have not improved, as envisaged, can be expressed both in mild and strong words. We observed that out of eight States the provisions of seven States Panchayat Acts in the Scheduled Areas (except Bihar) have been amended in pursuance of the Extension Act of 1996. It may be added that Conformity Panchayat Acts of Maharashtra and Orissa are more or less in conformity with the Extension Act. In short, the functions, powers and responsibilities specified in the Extension Act have been assigned to either "Gram Sabha and Panchayat" or "Gram Sabha or Panchayat", except importantly the one relating to following the pattern of the Sixth Schedule in administrative arrangements at the district level.

The Rajasthan Ordinance lacks direction and does not fully reflect the contents and spirit of the Extension Act. All these aspects have been evaluated in this study. *Chapter I* gives the historical perspective; *Chapter II* discusses the implementation of the Panchayats (Extension to the Scheduled Areas) Act, 1996, with field study results in Maharashtra and Orissa, and to a limited extent in Rajasthan; *Chapter III* narrates the comparative analysis of the implementation of the provisions in the Extension Act, 1996, and conformity State Panchayat Acts; *Chapter IV* contains conclusions and recommendations.

I owe my heartfelt gratitude to Prof. Bakshi D. Sinha, who helped us in the project from its inception, and to Dr. Mahi Pal for his expert observations.

We, on behalf of the Institute of Social Sciences, place our observations, suggestions and recommendations for consideration of the Ministry of Tribal Affairs, Government of India.

We are grateful to the Ministry of Tribal Affairs for the comments on the draft report in the light of which the report has been finalised.

New Delhi

P.S.K. Menon
Project Director

Acknowledgements

While conducting the study on "Panchayati Raj in the Scheduled Areas: A Critical Study", we have had discussions with policy-makers, planners and officials of the Ministry of Tribal Affairs, Government of India; State Governments of Maharashtra, Orissa and Rajasthan. We thank them for their help and cooperation in providing data and information and discussing with us various issues and problems related to the study.

We gratefully acknowledge the cooperation and assistance extended to us, particularly by Dr. P.K. Mohanty, Director, Ministry of Tribal Affairs, Government of India, New Delhi, Mr. P. Hakim, Secretary-cum-Commissioner, TDC, Government of Maharashtra and Mr. R.D. Khoroskar, Director, Tribal Research and Training Institute, Pune, and to Mr. Arvind Bahera, Secretary-cum-Commissioner, Government of Orissa and for their unflinching support in the conduct of this study.

We would like to place on record our thanks to our field personnel, particularly Mr. S.K. Sevakari, Field Coordinator, Pune, who did excellent and meticulous work in Pune and Nashik districts; and to Mr. Nirakar Beura, Field Coordinator, Bhubaneshwar who did strenuous field work, inspite of inclement weather, in Harichandanpur block of Keonjhar district of Orissa.

We are indebted to Dr. George Mathew, Director, Institute of Social Sciences, New Delhi for his able guidance and constant support in completing this study, as per schedule.

We extend our sincere thanks to all the members of the Institute of Social Sciences, who helped us immensely, particularly to Mr. Madhusudan Nair, Administrative Officer for his gracious help in providing infrastructure facilities; Ms. M.S. Usha, our efficient Research Assistant and to Mr. P. Nandakumar, who typed the manuscript with efficiency, sincerity and devotion, and to Ms. Sapna Sharma, Mr. Krishnan Namboodiri and Mr. P.N. Kuttappan for the secretarial assistance, as also to Mr. Balwant Singh Rawat and Mr.C. Gopi and other supporting staff for all logistic support.

P.S.K. Menon
Bakshi D. Sinha

Contents

List of Maps

Executive Summary

The research project Panchayati Raj in Scheduled Areas : A Critical Study was sponsored by the Ministry of Tribal Affairs and was conducted by the Institute of Social Sciences, New Delhi during the period May 1999 - March 2000. The field work was done in Orissa (Keonjhar District – Harichandanpur Block) and Maharashtra (Pune and Nashik Districts – Ambegaon and Kalwan Tehsils) and also Rajasthan (Udaipur District - Girwa Tehsil). The study oriented on the present has as its real purpose the projecting of measures for better local self-government institutions in the Scheduled Areas of the country in pursuance of "THE PROVISIONS OF THE PANCHAYATS (EXTENSION TO THE SCHEDULED AREAS) ACT " 1996.

The tribal communities are traditionally well-versed in the regulation, control and conduct of their domestic, religious, socio-economic-political and judicial affairs through the combined wisdom of their leaders and village councils. The Constitution (Seventy-third) Amendment Act, 1992, incorporating many path-breaking provisions for effective local self-government practices, was not automatically made applicable to the Scheduled Areas (Article 243M) because of their unique characteristics and special needs as also recognising the special features of the Scheduled Areas and the tribal people. Subsequently, on the basis of expert advice as contained in the Bhuria Committee Report, 1995, an Amendment Act was enacted in December 1996 enabling extension of the Seventy-third Amendment Act, 1992, in a modified form to the Scheduled Areas.

The Report contains four chapters and follows a sequence. An assessment of implementation of the Extension Act, 1996, based on an analysis of the conforming State Acts and field studies revealed that :

- Gram Sabha has been recognised as the supreme authority for the implementation of Panchayat (Extension to the Scheduled Areas) Act, 1996 (Act 40 of 1996), but its status is mainly that of a titular body because of the absence of delegated financial and administrative powers.
- The customary laws, traditional and religious practices differ from tribe to tribe and vary from one village to another.
- The attempt should be to provide more autonomy and independence to the tribes, and not accentuate more isolation. Also, the customary laws, focussing on good administration and principles of co-existence should be codified.
- Literacy and administrative expertise are lacking at the Gram Sabha/Gram Panchayat levels.
- A village comprises the main village and its hamlets, normally inhabited by homogenous tribes in each such hamlet. But in a village, there may be more than one tribe and the different hamlets may also consist of different tribes. So the administration of the village through the Gram Sabha, and the implementation of plans etc. in consonance with customs and traditions through the Gram Panchayats may pose difficulties.
- For implementation of the plans, programmes and projects, the Gram Panchayats in Scheduled Areas, do not have adequate means and/or manpower to handle, and monitor projects like minor irrigation, as it concerns the interests of two or three villages.
- The acquisition of land for development projects is governed by the principle of common good and larger public interests. Sometimes the acquisition of land in one Gram Panchayat area may benefit another village(s). Such issues should therefore, also be considered by the Panchayat Samiti of the concerned village, apart from the relevant Gram Sabha.
- The financial, marketing and other supporting institutions under the Tribal Sub-Plan have not geared themselves to the needs of the Gram Sabhas.
- Some Gram Sabhas/Gram Panchayats were devoid of Gaotham Area.

- Gram Sewaks in Scheduled Areas are entrusted with the work of many Gram Panchayats and are required to attend to development works in remote villages and hamlets with frequent travel covering large distances resulting in neglect of some areas. In the Scheduled Areas, a review of Gram Sewaks' jurisdiction should be made.
- An analysis of gathered data indicated that the major problems faced by the people related to insufficiency of drinking water, lack of internal and link roads, inadequate health and educational facilities, veterinary dispensaries, sanitary facilities, soil erosion and water logging.
- Wherever NGOs have been working on issues affecting tribal life, there was awareness among villagers about self-rule ordained by Extension Act.
- In the villages where NGOs were working the non-scheduled areas were also affected positively, due to awareness about Gram Sabha.
- As the post of chairperson of all tiers of the Panchayats has been reserved for the Scheduled Tribe, irrespective of their population ratio in the Panchayat, there is dissatisfaction among non-tribals, in Rajasthan particularly, at Gram Panchayat level because they would not have Sarpanchship at any time.
- There are a number of State laws relating to money-lending, forest, excise etc. which have to be amended in the light of the Extension Act, and State Panchayat Acts.
- As per the Extension Act, prior recommendation by the Gram Sabha or by the Panchayat at appropriate level is required for granting of prospecting licence or mining lease for minor minerals in the Scheduled Area and granting concession for the exploitation of minor minerals by auction, but no uniform pattern has emerged across the States.
- Surprisingly, none of the State legislatures has made any specific provision for making the Panchayat an institution of self-government by providing adequate safeguards so that the Panchayat at higher level does not assume powers and authority of the Panchayats at the lower level and the Gram Sabha.

- The State Governments have not paid any attention to adopting of the Sixth Schedule Area arrangement for administrative structure and has left out this provision while drafting their Panchayat Acts to be in conformity with the Extension Act.
- The rationale behind Extension Act was to empower Gram Sabha to approve and sanction all matters pertaining to tribal society and economy. The role of Panchayats at different levels was merely to execute decisions taken by the Gram Sabha. In this respect State Panchayat Acts of Maharashtra and Himachal Pradesh are in greater consonance with the Extension Act.
- Relevant Acts of the State Governments need to be amended in order to fully implement the Extension Act.
- 'Hesitancy' and 'bias' in dealing with the poor and deserving, have to be tackled effectively in the development culture, if Constitutional obligations are to be fulfilled.
- A High Level Committee should be appointed, to report within a period of say, six months, the status of implementation of the Extension Act and conformity legislations in all the Fifth Schedule Area States. Further, a Coordination Committee consisting of among others, the nominees of Ministries of Tribal Affairs, Rural Development (incharge of Panchayats), Planning Commission and the Finance Ministry may be constituted to monitor the implementation of the provisions of the Act (both Central and States) in the Scheduled Areas, State by State. Thereafter, the Ministry of Tribal Affairs may make a situational analysis and decide the future course of action to implement the provision of the Extension Act effectively.
- The interpretation regarding vesting of ownership of Minor Forest Produce in Gram Sabha must be resolved.
- The State Governments should re-examine the issue of adopting the Sixth Schedule Area arrangement for administrative structure to be in conformity with the Extension Act.
- The State laws relating to money-lending, forest, excise etc. have to be amended in the light of the provisions in the

Extension Act.

- Coordination should be ensured in the activities of the TDCC/ ITDA/ ITDP/ Block/financial institutions and the Panchayats to ensure harmonious and balanced utilisation of resources (men, money and material) for achieving plans/ programmes/ project targets.
- Training and sensitization programmes for elected panchayat representatives and functionaries must receive utmost attention.
- The Gram Sabha/Gram Panchayats must be endowed with administrative and financial resources.
- It is essential to create awareness on the bad effects of consumption of liquor.
- In the Scheduled Areas, a review of Gram Sewaks' jurisdiction should be made.
- The infrastructure under Tribal Sub-Plan should be utilised in a coordinated manner to achieve the objectives of the Extension Act.

1

INTRODUCTION

Profile of the Scheduled Tribes

According to the Shilu Ao Study Team on Tribal Development Programmes (1969), broadly speaking, there are three principal groups of tribes in India. At one end of the scale we have tribes living in the vastness of the hills cut off from all contact with the outer world, who are still in the hunting and food gathering stage. They are found in pockets in South and Central India and in the Andamans. At the other end we find virile race of freedom-loving, politically conscious tribals in North-East India, many of whom, through the devoted efforts of missionaries for over a century, have reached a state when they can rub shoulders even with their most enlightened counterparts amongst the advanced communities. And in-between we see, in the vast tribal belt which stretches like a girdle across Central India, from Orissa (including Andhra) in the East to Gujarat in the West, tribals in varying stages of development. While dealing with this bewildering mosaic of diverse tribes it would be unrealistic to proceed on the basis of the assumption that the stage of integration with the rest of the community can be reached by the end of a certain plan period. The Study Team suggested that the aim of tribal welfare policy should be defined as the progressive advancement, social and economic, of the tribals with a view of their integration with the rest of the community on a footing of equality within a reasonable distance of time.

Without going into the dialectics and semantics of the implications of the term 'tribe', it may be clarified that for the purpose of socio-economic development as well as for availing of various benefits guaranteed under our Constitution (political and job reservations, educational concessions and special financial allocations etc.) the term used in the Constitution is "Scheduled Tribes" and they are scheduled as per provisions in Article 342. The criteria generally adopted to specify State-wise Scheduled Tribes (there is no All-India Scheduled Tribe list) are, those communities with geographical isolation, distinctive culture, primitive traits, shyness of contact with the community at large and general backwardness. About 250 tribal communities (excluding sub-groups, synonyms etc.) have been Scheduled in 25 States and 4 Union Territories. Scheduled Tribes have not been specified in the States/UTs of Haryana, Punjab, Delhi, Chandigarh and Pondicherry.The Scheduled Tribe population in the country is unevenly distributed. About 85 per cent of them are in the central belt extending from Gujarat and Rajasthan in the West to West Bengal in the East through the States of Maharashtra, Madhya Pradesh, Orissa and Bihar. Most of the remaining 15 per cent Scheduled Tribe population is accounted for by the north eastern and southern states and Island groups.

As per 1991 Census, the population of Scheduled Tribes is 67.76 million, accounting for 8.08 per cent of the total population. The female and the male population is 33.40 million and 34.36 million i.e. 49.29 per cent and 50.71 per cent respectively of the Scheduled Tribe population. The Scheduled Tribe female population of 33.40 million incidentally represents 8.20 per cent of country's total female population (407.07) million, while the male ratio is 7.82 per cent. It denotes the pattern of sex-ratio in the tribal and non-tribal population of our country where the ratio of females is more in the former group than in the latter. While the sex-ratio for general population, as per 1991 Census is 927 females per 1000 males, in the case of Scheduled Tribe population, the sex-ratio is more favourable in that it is 972 females per 1000 males.

The Constitution of India contains exhaustive provisions for safeguarding the interests of the Scheduled Tribes. Commenting on the adequacy of the Constitutional provisions, the Dhebar Commission (1961) stated that :

> "the Constitution arranged for the provision of resources and provided the required institutional apparatus. We feel so far as the basic framework is concerned it cannot be considered inadequate".

Scheduled Areas

Historical Perspective

By and large, the tribal communities in India, particularly till the attainment of Independence, have remained comparatively isolated. This enabled them to maintain an uninterrupted long tradition of a well-knit-cohesive social structure and value system. They also had viable self-governing local institutions. The traditional tribal bodies — tribal councils/tribal panchayats - are one of the oldest known institutions of a local self-government nature. Today, these traditional institutions have become inactive or lost their influence or have generally weakened in such areas and amongst such communities which have had continuous close interaction with other communities or where statutory panchayats have been introduced. Still, one can find even today the old system working in many tribal areas and communities such as the Gonds and sub-tribes thereof (in parts of Andhra Pradesh, Madhya Pradesh, Maharahstra); Bhils (in parts of Gujarat, Madhya Pradesh, Maharashtra, Rajasthan); Oraon (in parts of Bihar, Madhya Pradesh and Orissa); Santhals (in parts of Bihar and West Bengal). Their functions, *inter alia*, include deciding of social and religious disputes in the light of Customary Laws.

The object of the British Government's policy in relation to these tribal areas was visualised by the Simon Commission. The Commission realised that perpetual isolation from the main currents of progress would not be a satisfactory long-term solution and that it would be necessary to educate these people ultimately to become self-reliant. The Commission observed that "the responsibility of Parliament for the backward tracts will not be discharged merely by securing to them protection from exploitation and by preventing those out-breaks which have from time to time occurred within their borders. The principal duty of the administration is to educate these people to stand on their own feet, and this is a process which has scarcely begun".

The proposal for centralisation of administration of these areas was however, not adopted in the Constitutional Reforms of 1935. Under the Government of India Act, 1935, these backward areas were classified as EXCLUDED and PARTIALLY EXCLUDED areas. Excluded Areas were placed under the provincial rule of the Governor acting in his discretion and the Partially Excluded Areas were within the field of ministerial responsibility, the Governor exercised a special responsibility in respect of administration of these Areas and had the power in individual judgement to overrule the Ministers, if thought fit to do so. No Act of Federal or Provincial Legislatures would apply to any of these Areas, but the Governor had the authority to apply such Acts with such modifications as considered necessary.

The Cabinet Mission's statement of 16 May 1946 mentioned the Excluded and the Partially Excluded Areas as requiring the special attention of the Constituent Assembly. The Advisory Committee on Fundamental Rights and Minorities, consequently set up three sub-committees (1) the tribal and excluded and partially excluded areas in Assam, (2) the tribal areas in the NWFP and Baluchistan, and (3) the excluded and partially excluded areas in the provinces other than Assam.

Both the Committees, relevant to India recognised that the ultimate solution to the problem of backward areas lay in development, not isolation. They recommended that both in Assam and other Provinces it would not be prudent to leave the responsibility for the development of these areas in the charge of provincial governments with limited financial resources and competing claims. The Committee, therefore, made it the responsibility of the Centre to draw up schemes for the development of these areas and ensure that they were implemented by the Provinces.

The sub-committee on Excluded and Partially Excluded Areas in Provinces other than Assam did not find it advisable to abolish the administrative distinction between the backward areas and the rest of the country. The general position according to the sub-committee was that the areas predominantly inhabited by the tribal people should be known as "Scheduled Areas" (the intention being that these areas should be in a schedule to a notification and special administrative arrangements made in regard to them).

Constitutional Provisions

After discussion of the report of the sub-committee, the Drafting Committee adopted, more or less, the whole scheme recommended by these sub-committees. In the final form, the Constitution of India, *inter alia*, provides the following important provisions in relation to the administration of Scheduled Areas, in particular, and development of the Scheduled Tribes, in general.

(1) Article 244 (1) — Administration and control of Scheduled Areas.
(2) Article 339 — Control of the Union Government over the administration of the Scheduled Areas and the welfare of the Scheduled Tribes.
(3) Article 275 (1) — Payment of grant-in-aid by the Government of India to enable the States to meet the cost of such schemes of development as may be undertaken by the States with the approval of the Government of India for promoting the welfare of Scheduled Tribes or *raising the level of administration of Scheduled Areas* therein to that of the administration of the rest of that State.

Scheduled Areas

The term 'Scheduled Areas' has been defined in the Indian Constitution as "such areas as the President may by order declare to be Scheduled Areas". Paragraph 6 of the Fifth Schedule of the

Constitution prescribes following procedure for scheduling, de-scheduling and alteration of Scheduled Areas.

"6. Scheduled Areas – (1) In this Constitution, the expression 'Scheduled Areas' means such areas as the President may by order declare to be Scheduled Areas.

(2) The President may at any time by order—

(a) direct that whole or any specified part of a Scheduled Area shall cease to be a Scheduled Area or a part of such an area;

(aa) increase the area of any Scheduled Area in a State after consultation with the Governor of that State;

(b) alter, but only by way of rectification of boundaries, any Scheduled Area;

(c) on any alteration of the boundaries of a State on the admission into the Union or the establishment of a new State, declare any territory not previously included in any State to be, or to form part of, a Scheduled Area;

(d) rescind, in relation to any State or States, any order or orders made under this paragraph, and in consultation with the Governor of the State concerned, make fresh orders redefining the areas which are to be Scheduled Areas.

And any such order may contain such incidental and consequential provisions as appear to the President to be necessary and proper, but save as aforesaid, the order made under sub-paragraph (1) of this paragraph shall not be varied by any subsequent order".

Thus the specification of Scheduled Areas in relation to a particular State is by a notified Order of the President, after consultation with the concerned State Governments. The same procedure will apply while altering, increasing or rescinding any order(s) relating to Scheduled Areas.

The criteria followed for declaring an area as Scheduled Area are preponderance of tribal population; compactness and reasonable size of the area; under-developed nature of the area; and marked disparity in economic standard of the people. These criteria though not spelt out in the Constitution of India have become well established. They embody, broadly the principles followed in declaring 'Excluded' and 'Partially Excluded Areas' under the Government of India Act, 1935, and spelt out in the Report of the Scheduled Areas and Scheduled Tribes Commission, 1961.

In exercise of the powers conferred by paragraph 6 of the Fifth Schedule to the Constitution, the President after consultation with the State Governments concerned had by Orders called 'the Scheduled Areas (Part A States) Order, 1950' and the Scheduled Areas (Part B States) Order 1950' set out the Scheduled Areas in the States. Further, by Orders, namely the Madras Scheduled Areas (Cesser) Order, 1951' and 'the Andhra Scheduled Areas (Cesser) Order, 1955' certain areas of the then East Godavari and Visakhapatnam districts were de-scheduled. At the time of formulating and adopting the strategy of Tribal Sub-Plan (TSP) for socio-economic development of Scheduled Tribes during Fifth Five Year Plan (1974-79), certain areas besides the then existing Scheduled Areas, were also found having preponderance of tribal population. A review of protective measures available to the tribals of these newly identified areas *vis-a-vis* Scheduled Areas was made and it was felt that a systematic use of protective measures and other powers available to the executive under Fifth Schedule will help in effective implementation of the development programmes in Sub-Plan Areas. Therefore, in August 1976 it was decided to make the boundaries of the Scheduled Areas co-terminus with the Tribal Sub-Plan areas. Accordingly, Clause (2) of paragraph 6 of the Schedule was amended vide the Constitution (Amendment) Act, 1976 to empower the President to increase the area of any Scheduled Area in any State. Pursuant to above, the President has issued from time to time Orders specifying Scheduled Areas afresh in relation to the States of Bihar, Gujarat, Madhya Pradesh, Maharashtra, Orissa and Rajasthan. The tribal areas in Himachal Pradesh were scheduled on 27.11.1975. While scheduling the areas in Himachal Pradesh the principle of making the sub-plan and the Fifth Schedule Areas coterminous was kept in view. Thus, presently the Tribal Sub-Plan areas (Integrated Tribal Development Projects/ Integrated Tribal Development Agency areas only) are coterminous with Scheduled Areas in the States of Bihar, Gujarat, Himachal Pradesh, Madhya Pradesh, Maharashtra, Orissa and Rajasthan. The State of Andhra Pradesh, where the Tribal Sub-Plan areas are not coterminous with Scheduled Areas, has also furnished a proposal to this effect, which is under examination in the Ministry of Tribal Affairs.

Following Presidential Orders are in operation at present in their original or amended form:

S. No.	Title of the Order	Date of Notification	Name of State(s) for which applicable
(1)	(2)	(3)	(4)
1.	The Scheduled Areas (Part A States) Order, 1950 (C.O.9)	26.1.1950	Andhra Pradesh
2.	The Scheduled Areas (Part B States) Order, 1950 (C.O.26)	7.12.1950	Andhra Pradesh
3.	The Scheduled Areas (Himachal Pradesh) Order, 1975 (C.O.102)	21.11.1975	Himachal Pradesh
4.	The Scheduled Areas (States of Bihar, Gujarat, Madhya Pradesh and Orissa) Order 1977 (C.O.109)	31.12.1977	Bihar, Gujarat, Madhya Pradesh and Orissa
5.	The Scheduled Areas (State of Rajasthan) Order, 1981 (C.O.114)	12.2.1981	Rajasthan
6.	The Scheduled Areas (Maharashtra) Order, 1985 (C.O.123)	21.12.1985	Maharashtra

It is provided that any reference in the above orders to a State or to a district or other territorial division thereof, by whatever name indicated, shall be constructed as a reference to the State, district or other territorial division of that name as constituted on the date of notification of the Presidential Order(s) applicable to that State.

Though the Scheduled Areas are administered as a part of the State in which they are situated, the Governor is empowered under the Fifth Schedule to the Constitution to (a) prohibit the application of any Central or State law, and (b) frame regulation for the peace and good government of these areas. The regulations, *inter alia* may (i) prohibit or restrict the transfer of land by or among members of the Scheduled Tribes, (ii) regulate the allotment of land to members of the Scheduled Tribes, and (iii) regulate the carrying on of business as money lender by persons who lend money to members of the Scheduled Tribes. The regulations framed or Acts (modified where necessary) made applicable to Scheduled Areas in the various States mainly relate to regulation of land transfer and money-lending.

The other important provisions in the Fifth Schedule relate to (1) submission of annual reports by the Governor to the President on the administration of Scheduled Areas, and (2) Constitution of Tribes Advisory Councils.

It would thus be seen that even before the provisions relating to Panchayats in Part IX of the Constitution were extended to Scheduled Areas in 1996 in a modified form, very many constitutional provisions were available to the States to protect and promote the interests of the Scheduled Tribes in the Scheduled Areas. *It is a different issue as to how far these have been used, where and how effectively they were used. It is not the purpose of this study to examine such details and therefore we refrain from giving any comments.*

Bhuria Committee Report

The now famous 73rd and 74th Constitutional Amendments forming a separate part (Part IX) of our Constitution containing provisions for local self-government institutions for rural and urban areas were epoch-making events. The Seventy-third Amendment concerning Panchayats contained a provision under Article 243 (M) of the Constitution that excluded its applicability in respect of tribal dominated Scheduled Areas (Article 244 and Vth Schedule to the Constitution) and Tribal Areas (VIth Schedule). Eight States *viz.* (1) Andhra Pradesh, (2) Bihar, (3) Gujarat, (4) Himachal Pradesh, (5) Madhya Pradesh, (6) Maharashtra, (7) Orissa, and (8) Rajasthan have Scheduled Areas*. Four States, *viz* (1) Assam, (2) Meghalaya,(3) Mizoram, and (4) Tripura have Tribal Areas. Article 243 (M) of our Constitution provided that in order to make the provisions of 73rd Constitutional amendment applicable to Scheduled and Tribal Areas, with such modifications as deemed fit, the Parliament could make a law to the effect. As a first step towards enacting such a law, the Government of India appointed a Committee of Members of Parliament belonging to Scheduled Tribe communities and Experts under the Chairmanship of Dileep Singh Bhuria, M.P. from Madhya Pradesh. The Committee, known as Bhuria Committee submitted its Report in January 1995. The Provisions of the Panchayat (Extension to the Scheduled Areas) Act, 1996 were primarily based on the recommendations of Bhuria Committee Report. The report spelt out the following important suggestions.

(i) Most of the tribal societies in India have been practising democracy and have been characterised by an egalitarian spirit. Cognizance has to be taken of the indigenous institutions, leaders and ethos while considering democratic decentralisation in tribal areas.

(ii) Time honoured customary laws, usages and arrangements in tribal areas should be recognised and allowed to continue. Traditional tribal conventions and laws should continue to hold validity. Their harmonisation with the modern system should be attempted.

(iii) Panchayat Raj bodies in tribal areas should be made more effective and participative in the context of the foregoing. More than in the past they have to function as institutions of self-governance and development. They have to work for socio-economic goals for removal of illiteracy, ill health amongst people.

(iv) For attainment of the aforesaid goals, flow of adequate funds has to be ensured. Such funds should be utilised for

* Today there are ten States including Jharkhand and Chhattisgarh.

the purpose they are set apart and should not be diverted. Suitable financial mechanisms should be created for proper utilisation of funds.

The Committee made the following recommendations and observations:

(a) Article 243B (D) envisages three-tier Panchayats at the village, intermediate and district levels in every State except in States having less than twenty lakh population which may not have intermediate Panchayat. In tribal areas, the villages are scattered and population-wise small. Such small hamlets or habitations may have their own Gram Sabha. The Gram Sabha should be allowed to exercise its customary traditional roles in the religious, political, economic, judicial and other fields. A Gram Sabha may have a traditional village Council to perform these functions on its behalf. The boundaries of Gram Sabha should be determined not merely with reference to physical parameters, but more importantly in consonance with the social, ethnic parameters. Further, the Gram Sabha may consist of all the inhabitants of the village/ hamlet, but the village Council may consist of selected or elected or nominated persons in accordance with the wishes of the village people. In other words, traditional leaders, elders etc. should continue playing their pre-existing role.

(b) A number of hamlets or small villages may constitute a village Panchayat or a Gram Sabha or Anchal or Parha or Pargana Panchayat and its members may be elected. Similarly, the intermediate tier Panchayat and the district tier Panchayat may consist of elected members, the latter being known by the name of Autonomous District Council (ADC).

(c) The broad frame-design of the Autonomous District Councils contained in the Sixth Schedule of the Constitution in the four States of Assam, Meghalaya, Mizoram and Tripura should be adopted with suitable variations as the organisational structure of ADC.

(d) For the ADCs in the Fifth Schedule Areas, the legislative powers proposed are more or less on the same lines as in the Sixth Schedule though with some amendments. In so far as administration of justice is concerned, the traditional jury-based legal system evolved by tribal societies should be able to continue to function.

(e) Since the Scheduled Areas and Tribal Areas are accepted to have majority of tribal population, the different tier Panchayats therein should have a majority of tribal members. Further, both the chairman and vice-chairman should belong to STs.

(f) Funds as envisaged in Articles 243H and 243I may be made available to Panchayats in Scheduled Areas. In addition, their share of funds as per the first proviso to Article 275(I) and TSP should continue to be available.

(g) In order to prevent wrong financial practices occurring in the TSP field, TSP funds (whether relating to State Plan or Special Central Assistance or any other pertaining to different sectors of development) should be quantified and placed at the disposal of ADCs for distribution among the Panchayats in the district. Moreover, to the extent possible, the Central and State Governments should devise procedures for allotment of funds to the ADCs.

(h) Education and health sectors should be the first charge on the funds received for Panchayats in Scheduled Areas and notwithstanding any other provision, the Panchayats should have the power to appropriate funds from any other head for meeting this obligation.

(i) All Government servants and functionaries of institutions concerned with the functions of a Panchayat in the Scheduled Areas and located within its jurisdiction should be under its control.

(j) Article 243H enables the legislature of a State to pass law for authorising the Panchayat to impose taxes, duties, tolls and fees and collect them. Article 243I provides for State Finance Commission for distribution between the State and Panchayats of taxes, tolls and fees leviable by the State. The two provisions assure Panchayats funds for carrying out their functions and this could be applicable to Panchayats in Scheduled Areas and Tribal Areas also. Additional funds under Article 275 (1) of the Constitution and Tribal Sub-Plan are available for tribal development purposes. All these funds should be placed at the disposal of the District Councils. The District Councils should thereafter distribute the funds among the intermediate Panchayats who should make the distribution to the Gram Panchayats which will, in turn, make the distribution to Gram Sabhas. The Central and the State Governments should place funds directly at the disposal of the District Councils. This will cut delays and improve accountability.

(k) Many Tribes Advisory Councils (TACs) have been dysfunctional. Many have not held their meetings regularly and the contribution to policy making or monitoring implementation of tribal programmes has not been significant. Action should be taken to review the TACs and make them functional and workable. The TACs should also be able to deal with matters which they think are important, in addition to those on which their advice has been sought on reference by the Governor. The Chief Minister should be the Chairman and meetings of the TAC's should be held quarterly.

(l) Till some time ago a Central Advisory Council (CAC) existed to advise the Government of India in policies, plans, programmes etc. of tribal development and their implementation, monitoring, evaluation etc. In its absence, the Government of India is deprived of the experience of the Council and a number of important tribal representatives, social scientists, experts, retired administrators, activists etc.

The Ninth Plan Working Group on the Development and Welfare of Scheduled Tribes expressed the view that people's participation had to be viewed not only in the field of planned development but also from the political stand-point. Tribal elite and even commoners have felt that devoid of political power, socio-economic plans and programmes could make little impression. They felt that if their own representatives could steer the implementing machinery by being at the helm, better results in the field could be achieved. It is more to the point to refer to the manner in which ethnic aspirations for advancement and progress have been met so far by Jharkhand Autonomous Council and Bodoland Autonomous Council which have been created during recent past.

While the Councils operate at the regional or sub-regional level, at the district and sub-district levels the Panchayat structure should infuse vitality into the process of socio-economic change at the grass-roots level. Altogether, one can assert that a silent revolution is taking place in the country with positive changes.

The formation of the Ministry of Social Justice and Empowerment at the Centre, a couple of years ago, and the establishment of a separate Ministry of Tribal Affairs in October, 1999 under the charge of a Scheduled Tribe Member are symptoms of greater awareness among the political leadership to tackle the problems afflicting Tribal Affairs with a sense of urgency and understanding to yield tangible results for betterment of the tribal people and the tribal areas.

2

Implementation of the Panchayats (Extension to the Scheduled Areas) Act,1996

(An Assessment Based on Field Study of Maharashtra, Orissa, Rajasthan and Scheduled Areas of Orissa)

INTRODUCTION

The specific objectives of the field studies were to examine as to what extent the 1996 Act was able to establish grass-roots democracy in the Scheduled Areas in accordance with the ethos of the tribal people and spirit of the Constitutional provisions, keeping in view the following aspects:

(1) Whether the Panchayats in the Scheduled Areas in the States of Andhra Pradesh, Bihar, Gujarat, Himachal Pradesh, Madhya Pradesh, Maharashtra, Orissa and Rajasthan have been endowed with such powers and authority as may be necessary to enable them to function as institutions of self-government, as envisaged in the 1996 Act;

(2) If so, the details;

(3) If not, the reasons and comments thereof;

(4) The nature, functions and role of Gram Sabhas to discharge functions specified in the 1996 Act;

(5) To suggest measures to achieve the goals, envisaged in extending the provisions of Part IX of the Constitution; and

(6) To study all other related issues *vis-à-vis* Tribal Sub-Plan mechanism, administrative structure, etc. in relation to Panchayati Raj in Scheduled Areas and to make recommendations.

Approach and Methodology

As laid down in the project proposal, two States (out of eight), *viz.*, Maharashtra and Orissa were selected for field study. In addition, the situation in Rajasthan was covered by field study though in a limited manner. It was also decided to have detailed discussions with the concerned State and district level officials. In the States of Maharashtra and Orissa, 25 Gram Panchayats each were selected on the basis of purposive sampling.

In Maharashtra State in *Pune district* covering ten villages/ Gram Sabha/Gram Panchayats and in *Nashik district* fifteen Gram Panchayats respectively were selected. Six Schedules were prepared for collecting secondary and primary data and information besides discussion with the concerned State, district, block levels (refer Questionnaire I to VII). In Rajasthan, some selected Panchayat Samities were visited though the study schedules were not fully canvassed.

MAHARASHTRA

Area and Population

The Scheduled Area under the Fifth Schedule to the Constitution in Maharashtra is 24,291 sq. kms. and that of the Tribal Sub Plan 50,757 sq.kms. as against the State geographical area of 3,07,713 sq.kms. TSP area works out to about 16.5 per cent of the area of the State. The comparative figures of the State's population and the Scheduled Tribe population in the last three decadal censuses are given on next page.

The population figures clearly show that during the decade 1981-1991, the ST population, as a percentage of the total population of the State, was more or less constant. The main tribes in

Census Year	State's Total Population (in lakhs)	Scheduled Tribe Population (in lakhs)	%
1971	504.12	38.41	7.62
1981	627.84	57.72	9.19
1991	789.27	73.18	9.27

Source: Government of Maharashtra, Annual Tribal Sub-Plan, Tribal Development Department 1998-99.

Maharahstra are the Bhils, the Gonds, the Mahadeo Kolis, the Pawras, the Thakurs and the Varlis. There are 3 tribes *viz.* the Kolams (all in District Yavatmal), the Katkaris (mainly in Thane and Raigad districts) and the Madia Gonds (mainly in Gadchiroli District) which have been notified as Primitive Tribes by the Government of India for planning purposes under the TSP strategy.

There are 31 districts in the State and Scheduled Tribes population is largely concentrated in 14 districts mainly in the western hilly districts of Dhule, Jalgaon, Nashik and Thane (Sahyadri Region) and the eastern forest districts of Chandrapur, Gadchiroli, Bhandara, Nagpur and Yavatmal (Gondwana Region).

In 1975-76 the villages with more than 50 per cent Scheduled Tribes population were constituted into Integrated Tribal Development Projects (I.T.D.Ps) under T.S.P. There were 16 such Government of India approved I.T.D.Ps. Subsequently, the villages where the tribal population was only marginally less than 50 per cent were also constituted into additional I.T.D.Ps by the State Government and these were called the Additional Tribal Sub-Plan (ATSP) Blocks/Projects. There were 4 such State Government approved ATSP projects. Later, taking into consideration the scattered population of Scheduled Tribes in other areas and the educational institutions being run there, I.T.D.Ps were also sanctioned by the State Government for Mumbai, Aurangabad and Chimur (in Chandrapur district), making a total of 23 I.T.D.Ps in the State and 23 Project Officers (P.Os.) were in-charge of these I.T.D.Ps. In 1992 in view of the deaths in the Jawhar-Mokhada area of Thane district and the need to give closer attention to health, nutrition and employment issues, the tribal areas of Thane district were divided into 3 I.T.D.Ps instead of 2, thus at present there are

24 I.T.D.Ps with 24 P.Os in-charge of these I.T.D.Ps.

In the meantime, the Government of India recognised that all over the country, there were some small concentrations of tribal population outside the I.T.D.Ps. It was therefore, decided that in a pocket of contiguous villages having a population of 10,000, with 5,000 tribals, such villages should be brought under the Modified Area Development Approach (MADA) to TSP. Later, it was decided by the Government of India that clusters of contiguous villages having a total population of 5,000, with more than 50 per cent tribals therein should be constituted into a cluster/mini MADA. In Maharashtra, there are presently 36 MADA pockets and 21 clusters/mini MADA. There is, however, still considerable overlap between the ATSP and the MADA and mini MADA/clusters and the Scheduled Areas.

As a consequence of the reorganisation of the Tribal Development Department in January, 1992, the 24 P.Os's jurisdiction have been so determined that they cover all the tribals in the State — whether living in the ITDP, MADA, mini MADA/clusters or scattered.

According to the 1991 Census, out of the total tribal population of the State, about 49 per cent resides in the ITDPs, (*i.e.* Scheduled Area and ATSP), MADA and mini MADA clusters (Refer Map1,) and the remaining 51 per cent live outside these areas. The scattered nature of tribal population is thus evident.

It was envisaged that various plan schemes and services should be integrated at the I.T.D.P. level. But there was lacuna in the proper integration of plan schemes and services as well as supervision and accountability at the project level in the Scheduled Areas. The Tribal people had to approach several agencies for development needs as also for other matters, because *departments working in the Tribal Sub-Plan (TSP) areas were independent of I.T.D.P.*

In view of these problems, the State Government in the State Planning Board constituted a Sub-Committee in January, 1991 under the Chairmanship of Mr. D.M. Sukhtankar (former Chief Secretary of the State), which submitted its report in June, 1992. The Sub-Committee recommended (which was accepted by the Planning Department of the State Government) the Plan ceiling to the Tribal

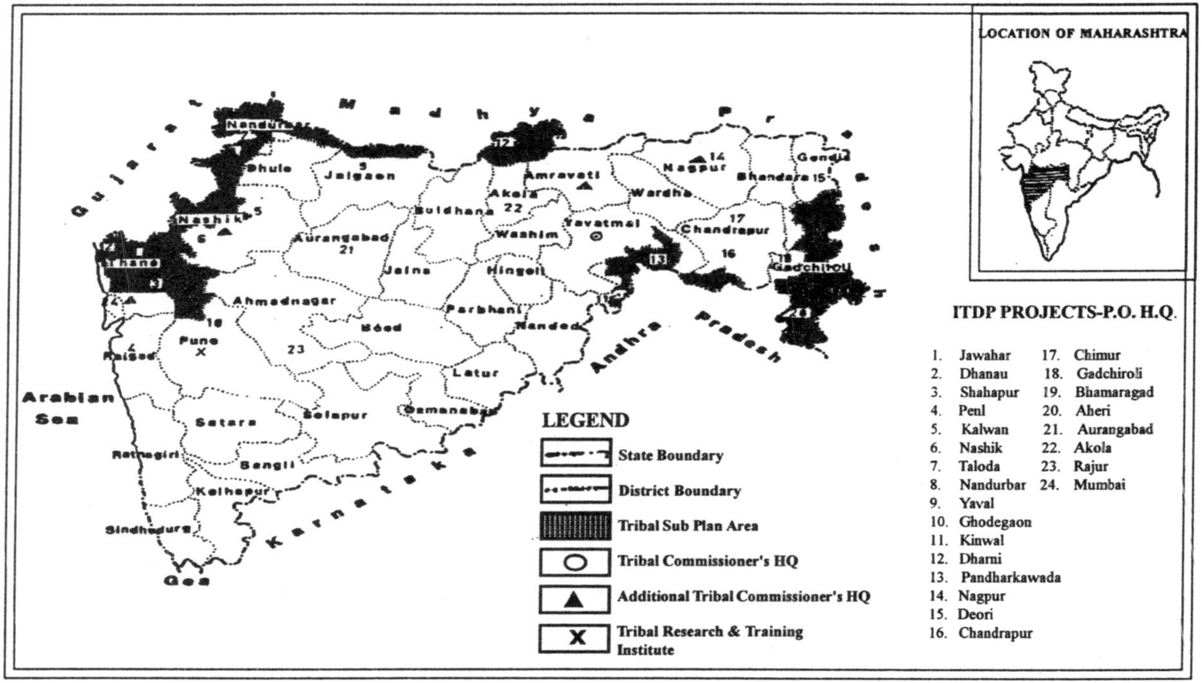

Map 1: Maharashtra: Tribal Areas

Development Department (TDD) for formulation of the TSP. The responsibility for finalising the TSP, within the plan ceiling, rests with the TDD, and not with the Administrative Departments of the State Government. The Sukhtankar Committee had also recommended that the major portion of the TSP outlays should go to the local schemes, which directly benefit the tribals, *e.g.* minor irrigation, soil and water conservation, rural water supply, link roads, maternal and child health etc.

The above procedure for implementation of plan schemes continued (under the provisions of Bombay Village Panchayats Act, 1958). After the Bhuria Committee recommendations and the 1996 Act, Maharashtra Government enacted and amended, as Maharashtra Act No. XLVI, on 29th December 1997, which endows upon the Panchayats in the Scheduled Areas the powers to function as Self-Government institutions.

The powers and duties of Gram Sabha in the Scheduled Areas in Maharashtra are as follows :

(i) to safeguard and preserve the traditions and customs of the tribals, their cultural identity, community resources and the customary mode of dispute resolution;

(ii) to approve the plans, programmes and projects to be implemented by the Panchayat for social and economic development before such plans, programmes and projects are taken up for implementation by such Panchayat;

(iii) to issue to the Panchayat utilisation certificate of funds by that Panchayat for the plans, programmes and projects referred to in clause (ii);

(iv) to identify and select persons as beneficiaries under the poverty alleviation and similar other programmes or schemes;

(v) to enforce prohibition or to regulate/restrict through Panchayat concerned, the sale and consumption of intoxicants;

(vi) to issue to the Panchayat with regard to the exploitation and regulation of trading of minor forest produce, subject to the provisions of the Maharashtra Transfer of Ownership of Minor Forest Produce in the Scheduled Areas, and the

Maharashtra Minor Forest Produce (Regulation of Trade) (Amendment) Act, 1997;

(vii) to make recommendations through Panchayat concerned with a view to prevent transfer or alienation of land in the Scheduled Areas and to take appropriate action through the Panchayat to restore any unlawfully transferred or alienated land of a Scheduled Tribe;

(viii) to make recommendations through the Panchayat concerned with a view to exercise control over money-lending to the Scheduled Tribes;

(ix) to make recommendations through the Panchayat concerned with a view to exercise control over local plans and resources for such plans including Tribal Sub-Plan.

Study Areas: Pune and Nashik Districts

In pursuance of the Maharashtra Act, 1997, which endowed powers to the Gram Sabha/Gram Panchayats, an intensive study was done with regard to the implementation of the provisions of the said Act and the Panchayats and their activities in 25 selected tribal villages.

In Pune District, ten villages were selected in Ambegaon Block (Tehsil) of Ghodegaon ITDP. In Nashik District, fifteen villages were selected in Kalwan Block (Tehsil) of Kalwan ITDP. In all 25 villages were selected on the basis of purposive sampling. (Refer Maps 2 and 3)

Village-wise area, tribal and non-tribal population and voters, by sex, both of Pune and Nashik districts are listed in Table 1.

Village-wise population of the Scheduled Caste and/Scheduled Tribe/OBC communities in Pune and Nashik districts, as per 1991 Census, have been shown in Tables 2 and 3 respectively.

Gram Panchayat-wise number of members elected by category and sex in Pune and Nashik district are listed in Tables 4 and 5 respectively.

The problems and prospects and basic services and facilities required in selected Gram Panchayats in Ambegaon Block of Pune district and Kalwan Block of Nashik district have been given in Tables 6 and 7 respectively.

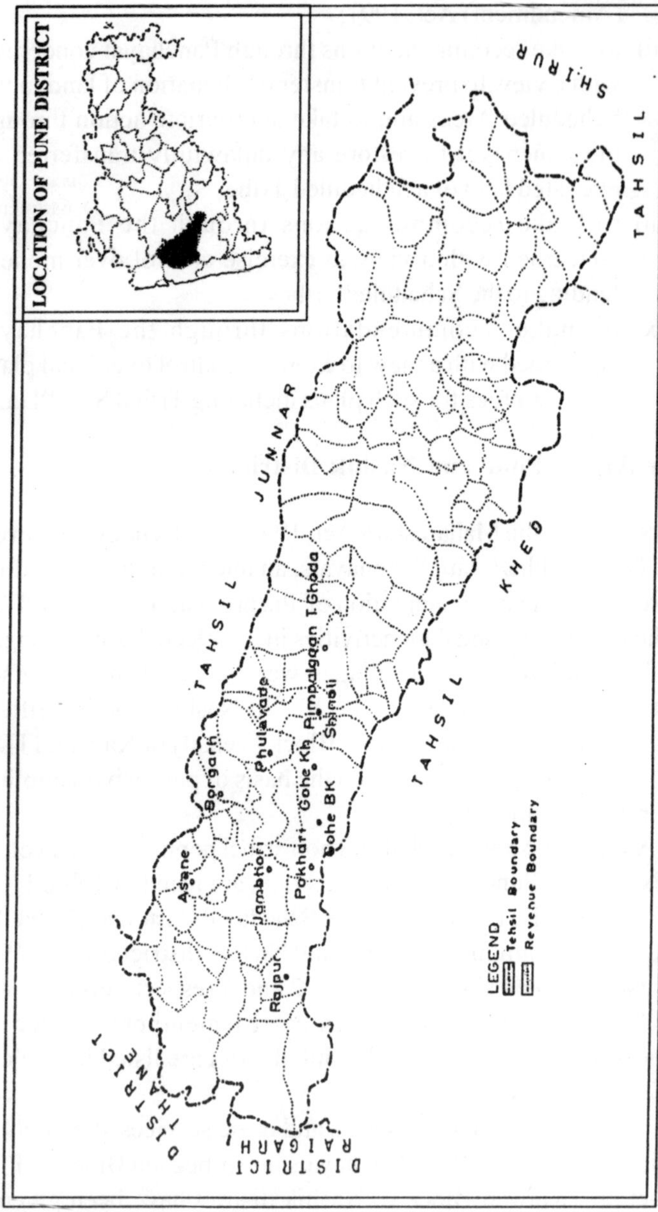

Map 2: Maharashtra: Tehsil Ambegaon District Pune

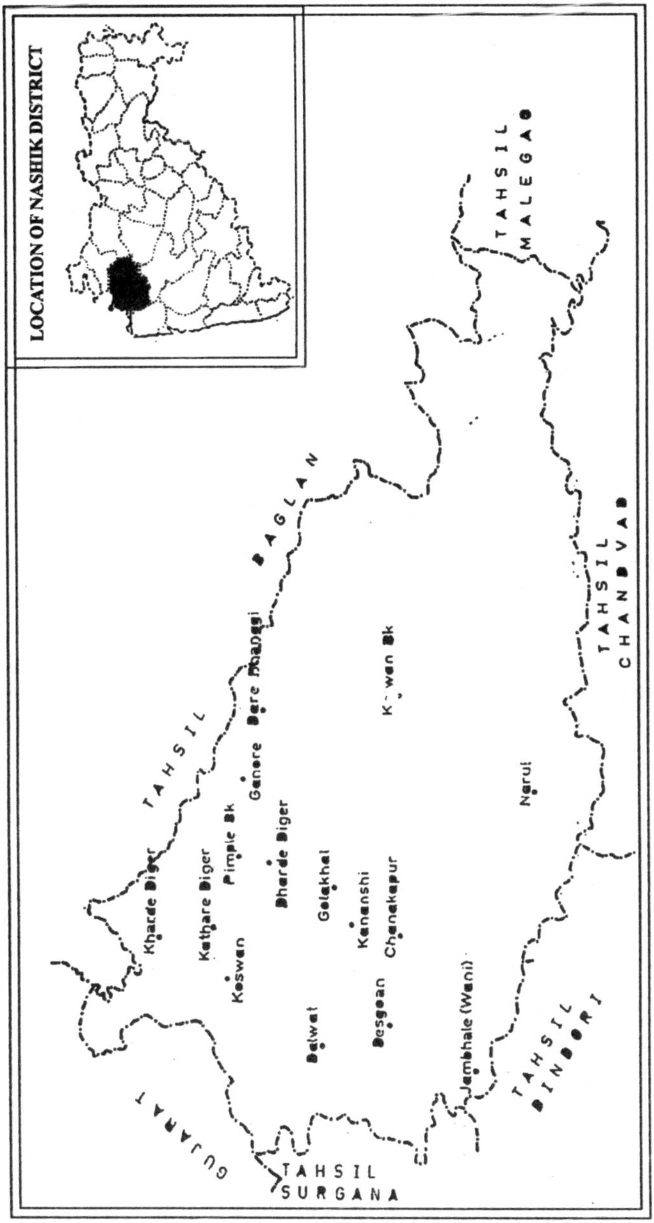

Map: 3: Maharashtra: Tehsil Kalwan District Nashik

Priority needs as stated by the majority of the people in each Gram Panchayat in Pune and Nashik districts have been listed in Tables 8 and 9 respectively.

Year-wise details of development works done in each Gram Panchayats of 10 selected villages in Pune and 15 villages in Nashik district have been laid down in Tables 12 and 13 respectively.

Implementation of Panchayats (Extension to the Scheduled Areas) Act, 1996 (Act 40 of 1996) in selected Villages/Gram Sabha/Gram Panchayats of Pune and Nashik Districts of Maharashtra

On the basis of analysis of the collected data and information gathered through structured schedules and discussions with the tribal people as well as the concerned officials at different levels, the following main observations are made.

(1) ***Gram Sabha*** has been recognised as the supreme authority for the implementation of Panchayats (Extension to the Scheduled Areas) Act, 1996 (Act 40 of 1996), but its status is mainly that of a titular body because of the absence of delegated financial and administrative powers. Gram Sabha has been given authority to approve plans, programmes and projects for socio-economic welfare for development of tribal people. But, actually the implementation of decisions taken at the Gram Sabha level are taken up by the Gram Panchayat level, which is an executive agency. It is observed that the tribal people are in minority in Gram Sabhas, because of migration of tribal families to the non-tribal and urban areas. *The Gram Sabha, therefore, should function as a guiding organisation in the Scheduled Areas and their recommendations must be made mandatory on the Gram Panchayats.*

(2) ***The customary laws; traditional and religious practices*** differ from tribe to tribe and vary from one village to another. Even in respect of the same tribal community, some tribes do not have any traditional management practices in regard to community resources. While intending to give due respect to

identify individual tribe and their customary laws and practices, one should not allow avenues for creation of disjointed groups of tribal society with conflicting codes of conduct. Therefore, the attempt should be to provide more autonomy and independence to the tribes, and not accentuate more isolation and drifting of the tribes. *Also, the customary laws, focussing on good administration and principles of co-existence should be codified.*

(3) ***Literacy and administrative expertise are lacking at the Gram Sabha/Gram Panchayat levels:***
It is observed that majority of nominated and/or elected members of the Gram Sabha or the Gram Panchayat and the women in particular are not literate. They do not possess knowledge about the functioning, procedures, rights and duties of Gram Sabha/Gram Panchayats. Hence difficulties arise in deciding or executing development works for the socio-economic development of the people in the area. *Training and sensitisation programes for elected Panchayat representatives and functionaries must therefore receive utmost attention.*

(4) A village comprises the main village and its hamlets, normally inhabited by homogenous tribes in each such hamlet. But in a village, there may be more than one tribe and the different hamlets may also consist of different tribes. So the *administration* of the village through the Gram Sabha, and the implementation of plans etc. in consonance with customs and traditions through the Gram Panchayats may pose difficulties. *A rapid survey of such heterogeneous tribal groups in a village Panchayat must be done by the district administration to chalk out plausible strategies for development.*

(5) For implementation of the plans, programmes and projects, the Gram Panchayats in Scheduled Areas, do not have adequate means and/or manpower to handle and monitor projects like minor irrigation, as it concerns the interests of two or three villages. Hence, *it is suggested that those development projects, which cover more than one village should be*

handled by the Panchayat Samiti or Zilla Parishad, but with the consent of the Gram Sabha of respective villages.

(6) The acquisition of land for development projects is governed by the principle of common good and larger public interests. Sometimes the acquisition of land in one Gram Panchayat area may benefit another village(s), for example opening of primary schools and health centres. The acquisition of land is followed by compensation. Such issues should therefore, also be considered by the Panchayat Samiti of the concerned village, apart from the relevant Gram Sabha.

There cannot be any difference of opinion about making the Gram Panchayat a self-supporting and self-governing institution in the Scheduled Areas. To achieve this goal the members of the *Gram Sabha/Gram Panchayats must be endowed with administrative and financial resources.*

(7) ***Maharashtra State Cooperative Tribal Development Corporation Ltd. (TDC)***

TDC has been given a free hand in plantation, procurement and sale of minor forest produce. This is a unique feature. *The TDC should also be given a free hand in procurement and sale of agricultural produce. It should, however, be ensured that TDC works with and for the benefit of the Primary Co-operative Societies in Scheduled Areas for percolating the benefits to Gram Sabha. The TDC should also have a networking to train the tribal people in each village.* With the responsibility of production, preservation, maintenance and restoration of the forest and agricultural produce, it is felt that the tribal people will be near self-supporting and the Gram Sabha/Gram Panchayat will be real self-governing institution.

(8) ***Other issues***

(a) *Grant of Prospecting Royalty and License Fee*

(i) For mining lease and minor minerals;

(ii) Grant of concession for the exploitation of the minor mineral, needs the sanction of the State Government; and

(iii) The financial, marketing and other supporting institutions under the Tribal Sub Plan have not geared themselves to the needs of the Gram Sabhas.

These provisions need review to be in consonance with the 1996 Act.

(b) *Prohibition :* The power to enforce prohibition by the Gram Sabha/Gram Panchayat cannot be effective because, the tribal people themselves are manufacturing and consuming liquor for generations, operationalised especially, if not as addicts, but to conform to traditional practices. They also go for illicit liquor when forced due to circumstances, and there is absolute breach of Prohibition Act in many tribal villages. *It is, therefore, essential to create awareness on the bad effects of consumption of liquor.* This education or creation of awareness should trickle down from Zilla Parishad and Panchayat Samiti levels.

(c) *Some Gram Sabhas/Gram Panchayats were devoid of Gaotham Area :* The declaration of the Gaotham Area and also the extension of Gaotham Area for a particular village lies within the jurisdiction of the District Revenue Administration. The procedure for declaration of Gaotham area in a village is invariably and inordinately delayed. Hence, *the procedure of declaration of Gaotham area must be looked into to render useful benefits to the local people.*

(d) *Heavy Work Load of Gram Sewak :* Gram Sewaks in Scheduled Areas are entrusted with the work of many Gram Panchayats and are required to attend to development works in remote villages and hamlets with frequent travel covering large distance resulting in neglect of some areas.

It is for consideration whether *in the Scheduled Areas, a review of Gram Sewaks' jurisdiction be made.* In the remote inaccessible tribal areas, one Gram Sewak may be entrusted with one or two Gram Panchayat, so that he/she may effectively manage and supervise development work and render assistance for promoting welfare of the tribal community.

In view of the existing problems, lacunae/gaps in the functioning of the Gram Sabha/Gram Panchayats in the

Scheduled Areas of Maharashtra, the following suggestions are offered:

(a) **Training of Gram Sabha/Gram Panchayat members :** The members should be trained in the following areas :

- Structure, powers and functions of Gram Sabha/Gram Panchayat.
- Panchayat know-how-meetings, quorum, agenda.
- Budget, accounts, functional aspects of planning, implementation, follow-up and monitoring.
- Socio-economic problems of the area and development programmes and projects to be implemented.
- Constitutional and legal provisions, in brief, for SCs, STs, women and children, including salient aspects of Panchayat Raj institutions.

Duration of the training could be between 10 days to 15 days in a village along with demonstration visits and the timings should suit the participants.

(b) ***Generation of additional funds :*** The members of Gram Sabha/Gram Panchayat should explore avenues to generate additional financial resources, besides receiving the grants based on population criteria and backwardness of the Scheduled Areas as well as low level of infrastructural support.

(c) ***Felt needs :*** An analysis of gathered data indicated that the major problems faced by the people related to insufficiency of drinking water, lack of internal and link roads, inadequate health and educational facilities, veterinary dispensaries, sanitary facilities, soil erosion and water logging.

To sum up, it can be stated that for the implementation of the Panchayats (Extension to the Scheduled Areas) Act, 1996 (Act 40 of 1996), the Gram Sabha/Gram Panchayats have their inherent limitations with regard to the implementation of programmes and projects. Considering the various factors, such as low literacy and economic backwardness, a change in the Scheduled Area has to take place with a lot of care and caution, where the pace of development is slow but transitional.

MAHARASHTRA

Table 1 : Village-wise area, tribal/non-tribal population and voters by sex

Sl. No.	District	Block	Name of the Village	C.C. No.	Geographical Area in Hect.	1991-Population		Voters 01.01.1998		
						Tribal	Non-Tribal	M	F	T
I.	Pune	Ambegaon	1. Asane	4	1074.00	1134	98	279	279	558
			2. Borghar	13	1734.82	1886	336	341	352	693
			3. Phulavade	24	1656.22	1323	314	379	346	725
			4. Jambhori	35	1649.00	1594	51	515	521	1037
			5. Gohe Bk	40	1286.00	2607	279	838	767	1605
			6. Gohe Kh	91	729.00	1015	37	317	323	640
			7. Pokhari	42	1075.00	1014	300	376	383	739
			8. Rajpur	45	1131.00	950	141	262	263	525
			9. Pimpalgao T. Ghoda	62	896.00	937	866	567	565	1132
			10. Shinoli	63	1748.00	1498	1839	920	940	1860
II.	Nashik	Kalwan	1. Khardi Diger	2	1789.90	2738	7	995	995	1960
			2. Kathare Diger	5	429.08	1066	13	447	463	910
			3. Koswan	8	1862.82	1293	—	379	422	801
			4. Dalwat	27	358.88	1583	149	454	434	888
			5. Kanashi	36	1757.05	1763	1511	879	886	1765
			6. Golakhal	37	894.73	1779	71	546	546	1092

(Contd.)

Table 1 : *(Contd.)*

Sl. No.	District	Block	Name of the Village	C.C. No.	Geographical Area in Hect.	1991-Population		Voters 01.01.1998		
						Tribal	Non-Tribal	M	F	T
			7. Ganore	49	881.08	1869	126	505	497	1002
			8. Pimple Bk	52	1125.34	1554	1	495	518	1013
			9. Dharde Diger	55	305.05	1098	9	457	461	918
			10. Darebhangi	62	1357.04	1033	18	313	338	651
			11. Chanakapur	97	433.30	1153	144	507	431	938
			12. Desgaon	101	969.04	1548	23	620	410	1030
			13. Jambahle (Wani)	110	1121.30	1376	30	450	454	904
			14. Narul	129	611.89	1590	59	519	530	1049
			15. Kalwan Bk	136	85.00	1952	11685	5225	4870	10095

Note: In many cases, the number of female voters exceeds that of males.
Source: Government of Maharashtra, District Statistical Handbooks.

Table 2 : Village-wise Total ST/SC/Others/Population by Sex (as per 1991 Census)

Sl. No.	District	ITDP	Block	Name of the Village	C.C.	Scheduled Tribe			Scheduled Caste			Others			Population		
						M	F	T	M	F	T	M	F	T	M	F	T
1.	Pune	Ghodegaon	Ambegoan	1. Asane	4	556	578	1134	33	25	58	18	22	40	607	625	1232
				2. Borghar	13	892	994	1886	5	8	13	155	168	323	1052	1172	2222
				3. Phulavade	24	671	652	1323	15	12	27	137	150	287	823	814	1637
				4. Jambhori	35	796	768	1594	—	2	2	36	13	49	832	813	1645
				5. Gohe Bk	40	1316	1291	2607	22	15	37	128	114	242	1466	420	2886
				6. Gohe Kh	41	473	542	1015	4	6	10	12	15	27	489	563	1052
				7. Pokhari	42	498	576	1014	3	5	8	162	130	292	663	651	1314
				8. Rajpur	45	479	471	950	6	3	9	73	59	132	558	533	1091
				9. Pimpalgaon T. Ghoda	62	571	366	937	6	8	14	311	541	852	888	915	1803
				10. Shinoli	63	912	586	1498	41	33	74	717	1048	1765	1670	1667	3337

Table 3 : Village-wise Total ST/SC/Others/Population by Sex (as per 1991 Census)

Sl. No.	District	ITDP	Block	Name of the Village	C.C. No.	Scheduled Tribe			Scheduled Caste			Others			Population		
						M	F	T	M	F	T	M	F	T	M	F	T
II	Nashik	Kalwan	Kalwan	1. Kharde Diger	2	1366	1372	2738	1	1	2	3	2	5	1370	1375	2745
				2 Kathare Diger	5	566	500	1066	2	2	4	6	3	9	574	505	1079
				3. Koswan	8	623	670	1293	—	—	—	—	—	—	623	670	1293
				4. Dalwat	27	809	774	1583	9	6	15	72	62	134	890	842	1732
				5. Kanashi	36	889	874	1763	114	116	230	636	645	1281	1339	1635	3274
				6. Golakhal	37	870	909	1779	27	36	63	4	4	8	901	949	1850
				7. Ganore	49	971	898	1869	14	11	25	55	46	101	1040	955	1995
				8. Pimple Bk	52	760	794	1554	—	—	—	1	—	1	761	794	1555
				9. Dharde Diger	55	549	549	1098	3	6	9	—	—	—	552	555	1107
				10. Dare Bhanagi	62	514	519	1033	11	5	16	1	1	2	526	525	1051
				11. Chanakapur	97	579	574	1153	22	22	44	53	47	100	654	643	1297
				12. Desgaon	101	756	792	1548	5	4	9	6	8	14	767	804	1571
				13. Jambhale (Wani)	110	691	685	1376	9	10	19	8	3	11	708	698	1406
				14. Narul	129	833	757	1590	7	7	14	25	20	45	865	784	1649
				15. Kalwan Bk	136	1024	928	1952	746	615	1361	5409	4915	10324	7179	6458	13637

Table 4 : Gram Panchayat-wise Number of Members Elected by Category and Sex
District: Pune, Tehsil: Ambegaon

Sl. No.	Name of the Gram Panchayat	Total No. of Members			Category: Scheduled Tribe			Scheduled Caste			OBC & Others		
		M	F	T	M	F	T	M	F	T	M	F	T
1.	Asane	5	2	7	5	2	7	—	—	—	—	—	—
2.	Borghar	6	3	9	5	3	8	—	—	—	1	—	1
3.	Phulavade	6	3	9	6	3	9	—	—	—	—	—	—
4.	Jambhori	6	3	9	6	3	9	—	—	—	—	—	—
5.	Gohe Bk	6	3	9	5	3	8	—	—	—	1	—	1
6.	Gohe Kh	5	2	7	5	2	7	—	—	—	—	—	—
7.	Pokhari	5	2	7	5	2	7	—	—	—	—	—	—
8.	Rajpur	5	2	7	4	2	6	1	—	1	—	—	—
9.	Pimpalgoan T. Ghoda	6	3	9	3	2	5	—	—	—	3	1	4
10.	Shinoli	7	4	11	3	2	5	—	—	—	4	2	6

Source : Based on field survey conducted in 1999.

Table 5 : Gram Panchayat-wise Number of Members Elected by Category Snd sex
District : Nashik, Tehsil. Kalwan

Sl.No.	Name of the Gram Panchayat	Total No. of Members			Scheduled Tribe			Scheduled Caste			OBC & Others		
		M	F	T	M	F	T	M	F	T	M	F	T
1.	Kharde Diger	7	4	11	7	4	11	—	—	—	—	—	—
2.	Kathare Diger	6	3	9	6	3	9	—	—	—	—	—	—
3.	Koswan	5	2	7	5	2	7	—	—	—	—	—	—
4.	Dalwat	6	3	9	6	3	9	—	—	—	—	—	—
5.	Kananshi	7	4	11	4	2	6	—	1	1	3	1	4
6.	Golakhal	6	3	9	6	3	9	—	—	—	—	—	—
7.	Ganore	6	3	9	6	3	9	—	—	—	—	—	—
8.	Pimple Bk	6	3	9	6	3	9	—	—	—	—	—	—
9.	Dharde Diger	6	3	9	6	3	9	—	—	—	—	—	—
10.	Dare Bhanagi	6	3	9	6	3	9	—	—	—	—	—	—
11.	Chanakapur	6	3	9	5	2	7	—	—	1	1	1	2
12.	Desgoan	6	3	9	6	3	9	—	—	—	—	—	—
13.	Jambhale (Wani)	5	2	7	5	2	7	—	—	—	—	—	—
14.	Narul	6	3	9	6	3	9	—	—	—	—	—	—
15.	Kalwan Bk	11	6	17	1	1	2	1	1	2	9	4	13

Source: Based on field survey conducted in 1999.

Table 6 : Gram Panchayat-wise Problems and Prospects in Ambegaon Tehsil of Pune district

Sl.No.	District	Block	Name of the Gram Panchayat	Major Problems of the Area	Prospects of the Area
I	Pune	Ambegaon	1. Asane	1. Kaccha Road 2. Insufficiency of drining water 3. Non Electrification of hamlets 4. Lack of transport facilities	1. Hirda processing units 2. Bee-keeping 3. Dairy development
			2. Borghar	1. Lack of link roads 2. Lack of hand pumps 3. Incomplete construction of public health dispensary 4. Lack of transport facilities	1. Vocational training centre 2. Dairy development
			3. Phulavade	1. Insuffieiency of drinking water 2. Kaccha roads	1. Dairy development 2. Horticulture 3. Lift irrigation
			4. Jambori	1. Kaccha roads 2. Lack of transport facilities 3. Want of irrigation facilities	1. Lift irrigation 2. Dairy development
			5. Gohe Bk	1. Lack of link roads 2. Lack of electrification of hamlets 3. Lack of irrigation facilities	1. Hirda–MPP–Processing unit

(Contd.)

Table 6 : *(Contd.)*

Sl. No.	District	Block	Name of the Gram Panchayat	Major Problems of the Area	Prospects of the Area
			6. Gohe Kh	1. Insufficiency of drinking water 2. Lack of link roads	1. Hirda–MPP–Processing unit 2. Domestic industries
			7. Pokhari	1. Insufficiency of drinking water 2. Lack of health facilities	1. Rice mill 2. MFP–Processing unit 3. Dairy development
			8. Rajpur	1. Insufficiency of drinking water 2. Kaccha internal roads	1. Hirda–MFP–Processing unit 2. Bamboo craft–Basketry 3. Dairy development
			9. Pimpalgaon Tal. Ghoda	1. Insufficiency of drinking water 2. No public latrines 3. Unavailability of training facilities	1. Lift irrigation 2. Dairy/Poultry development
			10. Shinoli	1. Insufficiency of drinking water 2. Hamlets not elctrified 3. Kaccha internal roads	1. Dairy development 2. Horticulture

Table 7 : Gram Panchayat-wise Problems and Prospects of Kalwan Tehsil of Nashik District

Sl. No.	District	Block	Name of the Gram Panchayat	Major Problems of the Area	Prospects of the Area
II	Nashik	Kalwan	1. Kharde Diger	1. No link roads 2. Insufficiency of drinking water 3. Hamlets without Anganwadis	1. Irrigation facilities through percolation tank 2. Bamboo work–Basketry
			2. Kathare Diger	1. Kaccha roads 2. No piped water supply 3. Soil erosion	1. Bamboo work 2. Dairy development 3. Soil conservation
			3. Koswan	1. Insufficiency of drinking water 2. No Primary Health Centre. 3. No drainage system 4. No veterinary dispensary	1. Bamboo work–Basketry 2. Rope-making
			4. Dalwat	1. No Gaotham area to hamlets 2. Kaccha internal roads	1. Sugar factory 2. Dairy development
			5. Kanashi	1. No Primary Health Centre 2. No office for Gram Panchayat 3. Kaccha internal roads	1. Rope-making 2. Domestic industries
			6. Golakhal	1. Insufficiency of drinking water 2. No link roads 3. Kaccha internal roads	1. Soil conservation, land development 2. Bamboo work–Basketry 3. Dairy development–Goatry
			7. Ganore	1. Extension of Gaotham Area 2. Insufficiency of drinking water	1. Irrigation facilities–PT/KT weirs 2. Social forestry–Grass plantation

(Contd.)

Table 7 : *(Contd.)*

Sl.No.	District	Block	Name of the Gram Panchayat	Major Problems of the Area	Prospects of the Area
			8. Pimple Bk	1. Kaccha internal roads 2. No piped water supply 3. No irrigation facilities	1. Dairy development 2. Vegetable growing
			9. Dharde Diger	1. Insufficiency of drinking water	1. Brick manufacturing
			10. Darebhanagi	1. Insufficiency of drinking water 2. No Gram Panchayat office 3. No dispensary 4. Kaccha internal roads	1. Wood craft industries 2. Irrigation facilities—percolation tank, KT weirs
			11. Chanakapur	1. Insufficiency of drinking water 2. No veterinary dispensary 3. Kaccha internal roads	1. Dairy development 2. Fishery activities
			12. Desgaon	1. Insufficiency of drinking water to hamlets	1. Lift irrigation 2. Dairy/Fishing
			13. Jambhale (Wani)	1. Kaccha internal roads 2. No culverts on Nala (stream)	1. Lift irrigation facilities through percolation tank/KT weirs
			14. Narul	1. No link/internal roads 2. No veterinary dispensary	1. Percolation tank 2. KT weirs
			15. Kalwan Bk	1. Insufficiency of drinking water 2. Kaccha internal roads 3. No link roads to new residential colonies	1. MIDC for small scale industries 2. Computer training centre

Table 8 : Gram Panchayat-wise important items of priority needs in Ambegaon Tehsil of Pune district

Sl. No.	District	Block	Name of the Gram Panchayat	Items of Priority Need								
				Drinking Water	Link Road	Health Centre	Irrigation Facilities	Employ-ment	Soil Conser-vation	Educa-tion	Samaj Mandir	Veterinary Dispensary
I	Pune	Ambegaon	1. Asane	2	1	—	—	3	—	—	—	—
			2. Borghar	1	2	—	—	3	—	—	—	—
			3. Phulavade	2	1	—	—	3	—	—	—	—
			4. Jambhori	1	3	—	2	—	—	—	—	—
			5. Gohe Bk	1	2	—	—	3	—	—	—	—
			6. Gohe Kh	1	2	—	—	3	—	—	—	—
			7. Pokhari	1	2	—	—	3	—	—	—	—
			8. Rajpur	1	—	3	—	2	—	—	—	—
			9. Pimpalgaon Tal. Ghoda	1	—	3	—	2	—	—	—	—
			10. Shinoli	1	2	—	—	3	—	—	—	—

Table 9 : Gram Panchayat-wise important items of priority needs in Kalwan Tehsil of Nashik district

Sl. No.	District	Block	Name of the Gram Panchayat	Items of Priority Need								
				Drinking Water	Link Road	Health Centre	Irrigation Facilities	Employ-ment	Soil Conser-vation	Educa-tion	Samaj Mandir	Veterinary Dispensary
I	Nashik	Kalwan	1. Kharde Diger	2	1	—	—	—	—	3	—	—
			2. Kathare Diger	2	1	—	—	—	3	—	—	—
			3. Koswan	1	2	—	—	3	—	—	—	—
			4. Dalwat	—	1	2	—	—	3	—	—	—
			5. Kanashi	1	2	3	—	—	—	—	—	—
			6. Golakhal	2	1	—	—	—	—	—	3	—
			7. Ganore	1	2	—	3	—	—	—	—	—
			8. Pimple Bk	1	2	3	—	—	—	—	—	—
			9. Dharde Diger	2	1	—	—	3	—	—	—	—
			10. Darebhanagi	1	2	—	—	—	—	3	—	—
			11. Chanakapur	1	2	—	—	—	—	—	—	3
			12. Desgaon	1	—	—	—	—	2	3	—	—
			13. Jambhale (Wani)	—	1	—	2	—	3	—	—	—
			14. Narul	1	3	—	2	—	—	—	—	—
			15. Kalwan Bk	1	2	3	—	—	—	—	—	—

Table 10 : Year-wise number of Gram Sabha meetings held and important decisions taken

Sl. No.	District	Block	Name of the Gram Panchayat	1998			1999		
				No. of Gram Sabhas held	No. of persons Attended	Important Decisions Taken	No. of Gram Sabhas held	No. of persons Attended	Important Decisions Taken
I	Pune	Ambegaon	1. Asane 2. Borghar			Details not available			
			3. Phulavade	1	51	1. Recovery of house tax 2. Construction of primary school building 3. Budget for 1999-2000 4. Construction of Samaj Mandir	1	53	1. Selection of BPL families for JRY 2. Selection of traditional craftsmen 3. Formation of Mahila Group
			4. Jambhori	2	52 61	1. Indentification of beneficiaries under Indira Awas. The Indira Awas Yojana aims at construction of houses and creation of micro habitats for SCs/STs/ freed bonded labourers 2. Schemes to be taken under JRY 3. Construction of school building 4. Budget for the year	1	45	1. Action plan under JRY 2. Identification of BPL families 3. Construction of Samaj Mandir

(Contd.)

Table 10 : (*Contd.*)

Sl. No.	District	Block	Name of the Gram Panchayat	1998			1999		
				No. of Gram Sabhas held	No. of Persons Attended	Important Decisions Taken	No. of Gram Sabhas held	No. of persons Attended	Important Decisions Taken
			5. Gohe Bk	3	127 162 127	1. Work to be undertakenly by Anganwadi 2. List of houseless families 3. Electrification of hamlets 4. Sanctions for the budget	2	143 150	1. Selection of beneficiaries for TRYSEM/IRDP 2. Action plan of JRY 3. Prohibition
			6. Gohe Kh	3	113 103 95	1. Construction of school compound 2. List of houseless families 3. Selection of beneficiaries for IRDP 4. Approval to the BPL families	2	110 107	1. Selection of beneficiaries for TRYSEM/IRDP 2. Action plan for JRY 3. New drainage work
			7. Pokhari	2	90 85	1. Selection of families for IRDP/TRYSEM 2. Identification of beneficiaries for Indira Awas	1	62	1. Action plan for JRY 2. Revision of house tax

(Contd.)

Table 10 : (Contd.)

Sl. No.	District	Block	Name of the Gram Panchayat	1998			1999		
				No. of Gram Sabhas	No. of persons Attended	Important Decisions Taken	No. of Gram Sabhas	No. of persons Attended	Important Decisions Taken
						3. Selection of families for village craftsman training 4. Construction of private laterine			
			8. Rajpur	3	45 70 72	1. New schemes under JRY 2. Selection of BPL families 3. Review of work done	2	90 77	1. Information about schemes newly introduced 2. New schemes under JRY 3. Approval of families under BPL and Indira Awas scheme
			9. Pimpalgaon	3	32 19 33	1. Selection of beneficiaries under Indira Awas 2. Schemes to be under-taken JRY	1	118	1. Action plan of JRY 2. Selection of beneficiaries under Indira Awas

(Contd.)

Table 10 : (*Contd.*)

Sl. No.	District	Block	Name of the Gram Panchayat	1998			1999		
				No. of Gram Sabhas held	No. of persons Attended	Important Decisions Taken	No. of Gram Sabhas held	No. of persons Attended	Important Decisions Taken
						3. Review of work done 4. Review of progress of work done			3. Approval of identification of BPL families 4. Selection of families for TRYSEM
			10. Shinoli	2	101 104	1. Programme finalisation under JRY 2. Construction of houses for houseless families 3. Gram Abhiyan	1	110	1. Selection of beneficiaries for IRDP 2. Review of work under JRY 3. Selection of beneficiaries under Indira Awas

(*Contd.*)

Table 11 : Year-wise number of Gram Sabha meetings held and important decisions taken

Sl. No.	District	Block	Name of the Gram Panchayat	1998			1999		
				No. of Gram Sabhas held	No. of persons Attended	Important Decisions Taken	No. of Gram Sabhas held	No. of persons Attended	Important Decisions Taken
1	2	3	4	5	6	7	8	9	10
I	Nashik	Kalwan	1. Kharde Diger	3	103 197 51	1. Action plan under JRY 2. Selection of beneficiaries for Indira Awas	3	101 149 105	1. Demand of house tax 2. Problems of sanitation and drainage 3. Selection of beneficiaries for Jivan Dhara
			2. Kathare Diger	3	101 100 110	1. House tax demand 2. Selection of beneficiaries under Jivan Dhara/Indira Awas 3. Approval of the list of BPL families	2	108 107	1. Action plan of JRY 2. Selection of beneficiaries under Indira Awas TRYSEM
			3. Koswan	3	115 89 102	1. Selection of beneficiaries under IRDP 2. BPL families survey results	2	105 78	1. Action Plan under JRY 2. Identification of BPL families 3. Drainage scheme

Contd.

Table 11 : *(Contd.)*

1	2	3	4	5	6	7	8	9	10
			4. Dalwat	4	91 107 95 106	1. Sanction to previous expenditure 2. Action plan–JRY 3. Selection of BPL beneficiaries for Jivan Dhara, Indira Awas	3	79 137 104	1. Sanction to previous expenditure 2. Selection of beneficiaries for Indira Awas TSP programmes
			5. Kanashi	4	101 140 107 119	1. Selection of beneficiaries under Indira Awas, JRY 2. Sanction to school room construction 3. Primary School Committee (appointment)	3	124 110 118	1. Proposal of Jivan Dhara 2. Selection of beneficiaries under Indira Awas 3. Approval to previous expenditure
			6. Golakhal	3	93 110 80	1. Action plan–JRY 2. Confirmation of list of BPL families 3. Indira Awas beneficiaries	1	60	1. Selection of beneficiaries under Indira Awas
			7. Ganore	4	90 87 105 97	1. Action plan–JRY 2. Review of work done 3. Budget for the next year	3	80 101 105	1. List of BPL families 2. Demand of house tax 3. Review of work done

Contd.

Table 11 : *(Contd.)*

1	2	3	4	5	6	7	8	9	10
			8. Pimple Bk	.3	104 70 106	1. Action plan–JRY 2. Selection of beneficiaries of Indira Awas 3. Sanction to BPL families	2	25 101 .	1. Sanction to previous expenditure 2. Selection of beneficiaries for Indira Awas IRDP
			9. Dharde Diger	3	100 70 101	1. Action plan–JRY 2. Selection of Indira Awas beneficiaries 3. BPL families confirmation	3	80 100 90	1. Govt. schemes 2. Identification of BPL families 3. Action plan–JRY
			10. Darebhanagi	3	86 53 97	1. Action plan–JRY 2. House tax demand 3. Selection of beneficiaries for Indira Awas	3	64 135 78	1. Action plan JRY 2. Sanction to previous expenditure
			11. Chanakapur	4	91 101 107 102	1. Action plan–JRY 2. BPL survey 97-98 3. Gram Abhiyan	3	71 91 71	1. Samaj Mandir construction 2. Water tax/house tax demand 3. IRDP beneficiaries selection

Contd.

Table 11 : (*Contd.*)

1	2	3	4	5	6	7	8	9	10
			12. Desgaon	–	–	–	2	107	1. Births/deaths registration 2. Identification of beneficiaries for TRYSEM/village artisan 3. Identification of BPL families
			13. Jambhale (Wani)	5	27 110 28 103 42	1. Review of development works 2. Sanction to previous expenditure 3. Action plan–JRY	2	103 49	1. Selection of families under Indira Awas/ TRYSEM/Jivan Dhara 2. New schemes of Government
			14. Narul	3	115 72 120	1. Action plan–JRY 2. Selection of beneficiaries for Indira Awas	3	110 80 91	1. House tax demand 2. BPL families selection 3. Selection of beneficiaries for Indira Awas, IRDP

(*Contd.*)

Table 11 : (*Contd.*)

1	2	3	4	5	6	7	8	9	10
			15. Kalwan Bk	3	25 97 112	1. House tax demand 2. Confirmation of BPL families 3. Budget sanction 4. Selection of beneficiaries under Indira Awas	2	101 102	1. Selection of BPL families for IRDP 2. House tax demand finalisation 3. Action plan–JRY

Comments : The information compiled Tables 10 and 11 brings out that the Gram Sabhas have taken the decisions in the following matters.

1. Work to be undertaken under Jawahar Rojgar Yojana.
2. Selection of beneficiaries under Indira Awas, IRDP and TRYSEM/Jivan Dhara Schemes.
3. Confirmation of beneficiary list of BPL families.
4. Demand of house tax.
5. Review of previous work done.
6. Sanction to the previous expenditure.
7. Construction of School Buildings, Samaj Mandir etc.
8. Formation of Mahila Groups.
9. List of houseless families.
10. Prohibition.
11. Gram Abhiyan.
12. Information about new schemes introduced by the Government as a policy matter.
13. As regards the attendance, it can be stated that a majority of people showed interest in the subjects handled by the Gram Sabha and they were largely attended by the villagers.

Table 12 : Year-wise details of work done in each Gram Panchayat in Ambegaon Tehsil, District Pune

S.No.	District	Block	Name of the Gram Panchayat	Year-wise details of work done 1997	1998	1999
I	Pune	Ambegaon	1. Asane	1. Repairs to hand pumps 2. Construction of link road	— —	— —
			2. Borghar		Details not available	
			3. Phulavade	1. Construction of two water tank numbers 2. Construction of primary school 3. Construction of Anganwadi		1. Anganwadi class-room 2. Indira Awas Yojana houses 3. Seven private latrines
			4. Jambhori	1. Constructed 27 houses under Indira Awas 2. Supply of bullock carts	1. Anganwadi rooms 2. Constructed 6 houses under Indira Awas	1. Samaj Mandir 2. Primary School classrooms constructed
			5. Gohe Bk.	1. Link roads	1. Public reading rooms (library hall)	1. Primary school building 2. Approach road 1 km.
			6. Gohe Kh.	No work undertaken	1. Drainage work 2. Anganwadi class rooms	1. Gram Panchayat office 2. Drainage

(Contd.)

Table 12 : *(Contd.)*

S.No.	District	Block	Name of the Gram Panchayat	Year-wise details of work done 1997	1998	1999
			7. Pokhari	1. Construction of lakes 2. Link roads	1. Public latrines	1. Link roads hamlets
			8. Rajpur	1. One classroom 2. 44 private latrines	1. Construction of one class room	1. 3 private laterines
			9. Pimpalgaon (Tal. Ghoda)	1. Constructed 10 houses under Indira Awas 2. 20 private latrines	1. 3 house constructed under Indira Awas 2. Construction of new road 3. Installed 2 hand pumps	
			10. Shinoli	1. Compound wall of primany school 2. 25 private latrines	1. 40 private latrines constructed 2. Constructed 2 houses under Indira Awas	1. Constructed 2 houses under Indira Awas

Comments : From the above information it is indicated that the Gram Panchayats have carried out the work *viz*. construction of primary school classrooms, anganwadi classrooms, Gram Panchayat Office, Samaj Mandir, link roads, drainage work, water tanks, houses under Indira Awas, private latrines etc. during the years under study.

Table 13 : Year - wise details of work done in each Gram Panchayat in Kalwan Tahsil, District Nashik

Sl.No.	District	Block	Name of the Gram Panchayat	Year-wise details of work done 1997	1998	1999
II	Nashik	Kalwan	1. Kharde Diger	1. Samaj Mandir 2. Wells 3. 8 houses under Indira Awas 4. 30 private latrines	1. School classrooms 2. 40 houses under Indira Awas 3.36 private latrines	1. Samaj Mandir 2. Drainage work
			2. Kathare Diger	1. Drainage work 2. School classroom 3. 12 houses under Indira Awas 4. 45 private latrines	1. School classroom 2. 23 private latrines	
			3. Koswan	1. Samaj Mandir 2. School classroom (Anganwadi)	1. Repairs to school building 2. 12 houses under Indira Awas	
			4. Dalwat	1. Gram Panchayat Office 2. Primary school at Dalwat 3. 12 houses under Indira Awas	1. 12 houses under Indira Awas 2. Anganwadi	1. 44 houses under Indira Awas 2. Gram Sankar Centre
			5. Kanashi	1. Primary school building 2. 70 private latrines 3. 16 houses under Indira Awas	1. Primary school building 2. 60 private latrines 3. 18 houses under Indira Awas	

(Contd.)

Table 13 : *(Contd.)*

Sl.No.	District	Block	Name of the Gram Panchayat	Year-wise details of work done 1997	1998	1999
			6. Golakhal	1. One classroom (primary school)	1. Samaj Mandir at Deulpada 2. Internal roads 3. 14 houses – Indira Awas	
			7. Gonare	1. 10 houses – Indira Awas 2. 60 private latrines	1. 10 houses – Indira Awas 2. 40 private latrines 3. Primary school building 4. Pipeline – water supply 5. Water tank 6. Kaccha roads to hamlet	
			8. Pimple Bk	1. Primary school wall compound 2. 60 private latrines 3. Roads 4. 12 wells – Jivan Dhara	1. Anganwadi 2. Compound wall 3. 8 houses – Indira Awas 4. 11 private latrines completed	
			9. Dharde Diger	1. School classrooms 2. Water tank	1. Electric motor pump/pipeline 2. Samaj Mandir	
			10. Darebhanagi	1. 10 houses under Indira Awas 2. Anganwadi room 3. Mini water supply scheme	1. 20 private latrines 2. 10 houses – Indira Awas	

(Contd.)

Table 13 : *(Contd.)*

Sl. No.	District	Block	Name of the Gram Panchayat	Year-wise details of work done 1997	1998	1999
			11. Chanakapur	1. Drainage work 2. 8 houses – Indira Awas 3. 35 private latrines	1. Water tank 2. 39 private latrines	
			12. Desgaon	1. Primary school building 2. 10 private latrines	1. Primary school class-rooms 2. 5 private latrines 3. Supply of bullocks	
			13. Jambholi (Wani)	1. Drainage works – chinchapada 2. 12 private latrines	1. 6 houses – Indira Awas 2. Primary school building 3. 3 private latrines	
			14. Narul	1. 10 houses – Indira Awas 2. 40 private latrines 3. Water supply scheme	1. Water tank 2. 25 private latrines 3. 9 houses – Indira Awas	1. 18 houses – Indira Awas 2. 10 private latrines 3. Water supply stand post
			15. Kalwan Bk	1. Water tank 2. Internal kaccha roads	1. Drainage works 2. Water supply pipeline	1. No actual work started

Comments : The Gram Panchayats have carried out construction of primary school classrooms, anganwadi classrooms, construction of Gram Panchayat office, Samaj Mandir, link roads, drainage work. water tank, houses under Indira Awas, private latrines etc. during the years under study. Maximum work under private latrines and Indira Awas has been undertaken in this block.

ORISSA

Introduction

According to 1991 census, the total population of the State is 3,16,59,736 out of which the population of the Scheduled Tribes is 70,32,214, constituting 22.21 per cent of the State's total population. Population of the Scheduled Tribes of the State accounts for 10.38 per cent of the country's total tribal population. In terms of tribal concentration, Orissa features below only two States, namely Madhya Pradesh and Maharashtra.

The Scheduled Areas cover 69,613.80 sq. km.which is about 44.70 per cent of the total area of the State. Its total population is 88,71,071 out of which the population of Scheduled Tribes is 47,62,207 constituting 53.68 per cent, as per 1991 census. The tribal population of the Scheduled Areas is 67.72 per cent of the total population of the State as per 1991 census. The details of the Scheduled Areas along with its population are given in Annexure I.

The Scheduled Areas in Orissa are nearly coterminous with the Tribal Sub-Plan area of the State, except that Suruda Tehsil (excluding Gazalbadi and Gochha Grama Panchayat) of Ganjam district, which is included in the Scheduled Areas, is not under the Tribal Sub-Plan areas. Consequent to the creation of 17 new districts, the Scheduled Areas now cover 7 districts fully, and 6 districts in part, out of 30 districts in the State.

The welfare of the Scheduled Tribes of the Scheduled Areas in the State is being looked after in pursuance of Article 46 and Fifth Schedule of the Constitution. Schemes and programmes are being drawn up under TSP since the Fifth Five-year Plan for the all-round development of the tribals and to bridge the gap in the socio-economic conditions of these communities and that of others.

Tribal Sub-Plan (TSP)

There are 21 I.T.D.As (Integrated Tribal Development Agencies) and 13 Micro Projects (for Primitive Tribal Groups) under the Tribal Sub-Plan. Each I.T.D.A is headed by a Project Administrator (P.A.), an officer of State Civil Service Class-I rank and assisted by a Special Officer (SCS Class-II rank). P.As work under the immediate control and supervision of the District Magistrate and Collector. The P.A is the Member-Secretary while the local M.Ps, M.L.As, Chairmen of Panchayat Samities and other District Level Officers in charge of development works are the members of the ITDA Committee. Each Micro Project is headed by Special Officer under the immediate control and supervision of the District Magistrate and Collector. In each Micro Project there is a Governing Body constituted under the Chairmanship of concerned Project Administrator of I.T.D.A. (Refer Map 4).

Pursuant to the Panchayats (Extension to Scheduled Areas) Act, 1996, the State Government of Orissa amended its earlier legislations as (i) Orissa Grama Panchayats (Amendment) Act, 1997 (Act 15 of 1997); (ii) Orissa Panchayat Samiti (Amendment) Act, 1997 (Act 16 of 1997); and (iii) Orissa Zilla Parishad (Amendment) Act, 1997 (Act 17 of 1997) and this was notified in the Orissa Gazette dated 22nd December 1997.

The definition of Grama in the Scheduled Areas, according to the amended Act, is that of a habitation or a group of habitations or a hamlet or a group of hamlets comprising a community or communities and managing its affairs in accordance with traditions and customs.

As per Orissa Grama Panchayats (Amendment) Act of 1997, the *Gram Sasan* "shall have the power to approve the plans, programmes and projects for social and economic development before such plans, programmes and projects are taken up for implementation by the Gram Panchayat and identify or select persons as beneficiaries under the poverty alleviation or similar other programmes".

In the Scheduled Areas, the Gram Sasan shall be competent to safeguard and preserve the traditions and customs of the people, their cultural identity, community resources and customary mode of dispute resolution, consistent with the relevant laws in force and in harmony with basic tenets of the Constitution and human rights.

The Orissa Gram Panchayats (Amendment) Act of 1997

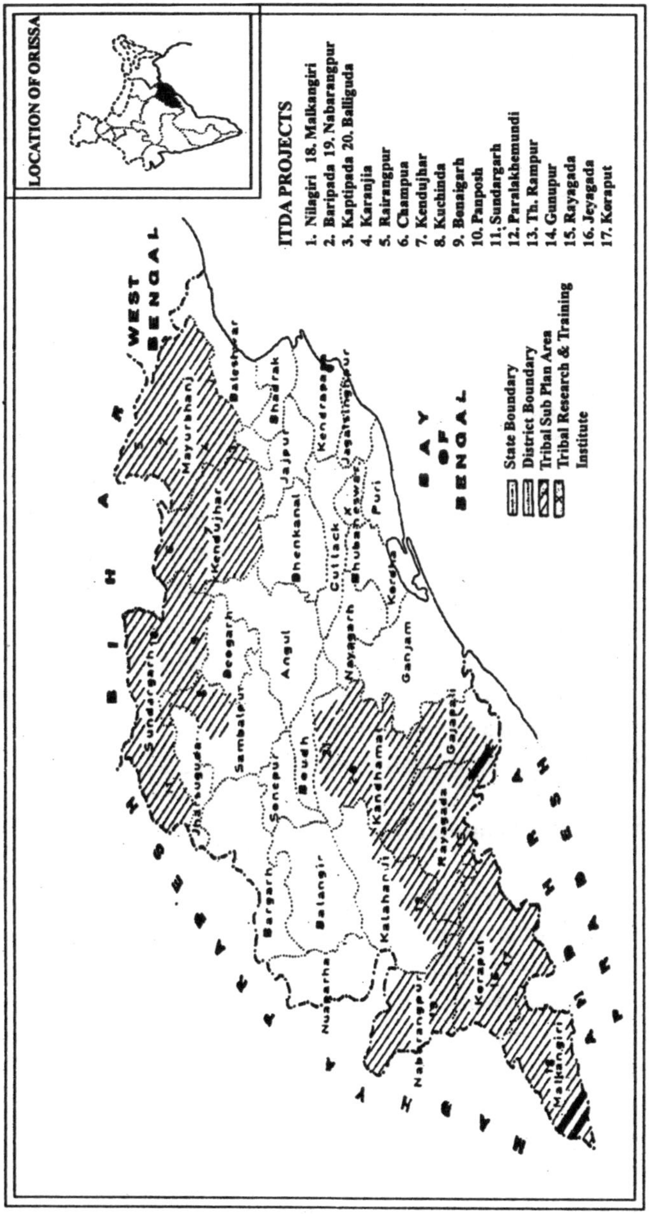

Map 4: Orissa: Tribal Areas

further states: Notwithstanding anything contained in any other law, in the Scheduled Areas, subject to the control and supervision of Gram Sasan, the Gram Panchayat shall exercise within its local limits such powers and perform such functions in such manner and to such an extent as may be prescribed in respect of inter alia the following matters, namely :

(a) enforcement of prohibition or regulation or restriction of the sale and consumption of any intoxicant;
(b) the ownership of minor forest produce;
(c) prevention of alienation of land and restoration of unlawfully alienated land of a Scheduled Tribe;
(d) control over money-lending to the Scheduled Tribes.

It is further provided (Section 9 (iii) of the Act) that "on approval of the Gram Sasan, the annual budget or, as the case may be, the supplementary budget or revised budget, the Gram Panchayat shall forward the same to the Subdivisional Panchayat Officer appointed by the Director, who shall be competent to examine the budget and shall furnish his comments to the Gram Panchayat which shall be palced before the Grama Sasan for consideration and finalisation with or without any modification as may be necessary".

Study Area: Harichandanpur Block of Keonjhar District

Keonjhar district covers an area of 8503 sq. km., which is 5.33 per cent of the total area of the State. For administrative purposes, the district is divided into 3 sub-divisions, 7 tehsils and 13 blocks. There are 244 Gram Panchayats, 7 towns and 2,127 villages in the district. Of the total area of the district, 30 per cent is covered by forests and about 36 per cent is utilised for agriculture.

The total population of 13.37 lakh (1991 census) in Keonjhar district is constituted of 44.51 per cent Scheduled Tribes, 11.5 per cent Scheduled Castes and rest 44 per cent O.B.Cs and other castes/communities. A decadal growth rate of 19.95 per cent (1981-91) was recorded. The density of population is 161 per sq. km. The district literacy rate of 36.72 per cent is lower than the State literacy rate of 49.09 per cent.

After discussion with the State, district, and block level officials and as per the norms and methodology of the study, it was decided to select 25 villages of Harichandanpur block covered under I.T.D.A. (Refer Map 5).

Harichandanpur block covers an area of 592.92 sq. km having 208 inhabited villages with 19,871 households. These villages fall under 18 Gram Panchayats. In the total population of 1,03,462 there are 55,133 people belonging to Scheduled Tribes and 7,707 belonging to Scheduled Castes (*i.e.* 53.55 per cent and 7.45 per cent respectively) as per 1991 census. The rest of the population of 40,562 (39.02 per cent) belongs to OBCs/other castes/communities. (Table 14).

For the present study 25 villages, 13 Gram Panchayats (out of 18 Gram Panchayats) in Harichandanpur block (Table 15) were selected. The details are given in Table 16.

The attendance data of members in the meetings of Gram Sabha in 13 Gram Panchayats during 1997, 1998 and 1999 were collected. It seems that after creating awareness among the members of Palli Sabha (or Gram Sabha), gradually the attendance of members in all the meetings increased from February 1998 onwards and continued during 1999. (Table 18)

During these meetings, the members of the Palli Sabha (Gram Sabha)/ Gram Panchayat discussed the major problems of each of the 13 Gram Panchayats and also of 25 selected villages along with the prospects for development works and socio-economic facilities to be extended in these areas by the ITDA's personnel and other concerned staff of Gram Panchayats, *but no substantial work was undertaken so far in the surveyed areas due to lack of funds.* (Table 19). However, after discussing with the members of the Gram Sabha/Gram Panchayats, the priority areas for development works and socio-economic facilities in 13 Gram Panchayats were spelled out which have been given in Table 20.

Assessment

(1) In Harichandanpur block, more than 90 per cent of the

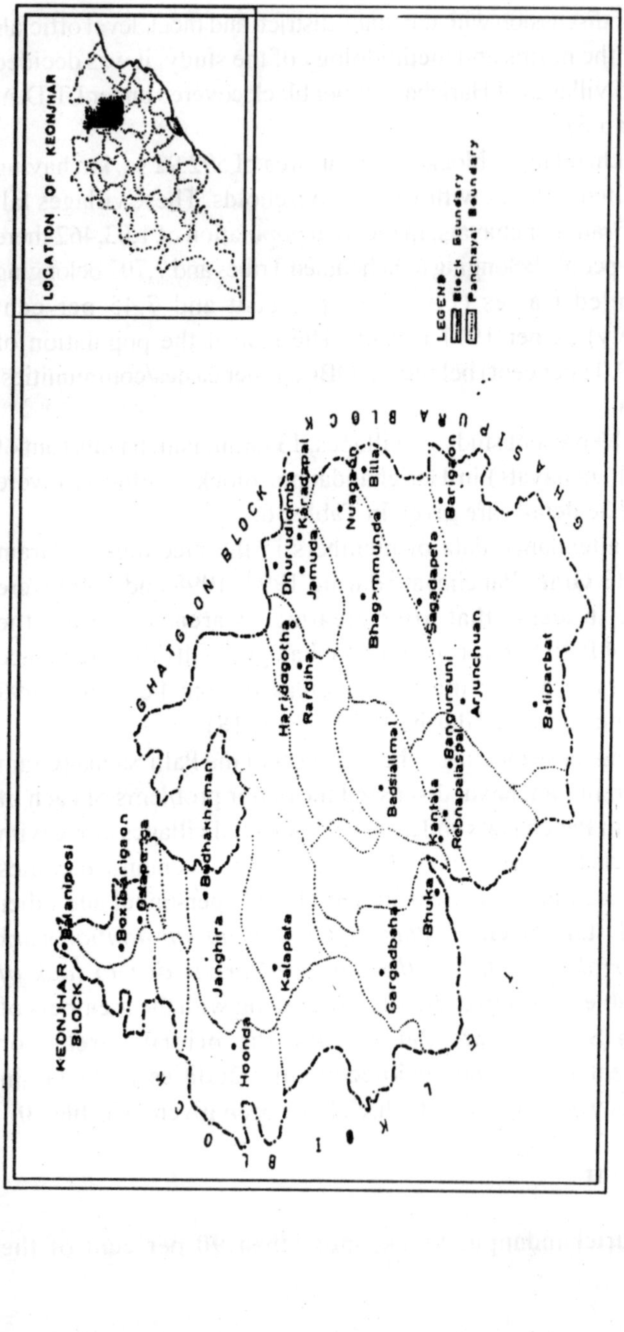

Map 5: Orissa: Harichandanpur Block District Keonjhar

Scheduled Tribes/Castes families are living below poverty line. The health condition of these people is very precarious for lack of support facilities, such as drinking water, transport, communication, roads (in fact only pedestrian tracks are found from village to village).

(2) The majority of the tribal people do not have any knowledge about the working/functioning of Palli (Gram) Sabha or Gram Panchayat . Even then, they are well organised in their villages and are functioning well under the traditional Panchayats, where disputes are resolved by their counsellor, as and when needed.

(3) The majority of the tribal people collect fuel stick, fruits etc. for their livelihood from the forests.

(4) They rarely attend meetings of the Palli Sabha/Gram Panchayat as they have to cover long distances (more than 6 km.) on foot for lack of bus or any other transport facility.

(5) Absence of the tribal people at the meetings is also attributed to the Panchayat officials (Gram Sevak, Sarpanch or Secretary) not informing them in time about the meetings. *Sometimes in order to fill the quorum of the Panchayat meeting the minimum required number of 25 tribal or non-tribal persons are collected, where matters of development work are recorded under I.T.D.P schemes for their implementation.*

(6) The discussions with the B.D.C, Welfare Extension Officer (WEO) and Social Activists in Harichandanpur Block and Branch Manager, TDCC, Keonjhar revealed that none of the officials were fully aware of the priority needs of the tribal people in their village/area, but plans, programmes and projects were being implemented on the basis of funds made available to them and developmental and socio-economic schemes were implemented in order to achieve the targets.

Suggestions

(1) *Panchayats (Extension to the Scheduled Areas) Act 1996 based on the Bhuria Committee Report should be followed in letter and spirit and reflected in the legislations.* The

Palli (Gram) Sabhas and Gram Panchayats should be endowed with powers for implementation of development and socio-economic activities.

(2) To mobilise tribal people and create awareness among them about their rights, duties and responsibilities, sensitization campaigns and regular training programmes are required.

(3) Intensive training programmes for the concerned officials of the district/block, panchayat representatives, the village leaders and ITDP officials need to be organised for the execution of plans, programmes and projects systematically.

(4) Financial and administrative powers should be given to Palli Sabha (Gram Sabha)/Gram Panchayat.

(5) TDCC should collect all types of forest produce from the tribals. Lease of forest produce to private parties should be stopped.

(6) The rights on land, forest and water should be given to the tribal people so that they may administer these resources judicially through their Palli/village Council (Gram Sabha).

(7) The tribal people living in reserved forest areas should not be displaced without suitable rehabilitation package.

(8) Effective coordination is needed in the activities of the TDCC, ITDA, Block financial institutions and Panchayats. This will ensure harmonious balanced utilisation of resources (men, money and material) for proper implementation of plans, programmes and projects in Harichandanpur block.

ORISSA

Table 14 : Gram Panchayat-wise Population Harichandanpur Block

Sl. No.	Name of the Gram Panchayat	Household No.	Total	Poplation		
				SC	ST	OBC
1.	Tangiripara	1899	8979	525	6908	1546
2.	Sagadepeta	752	4692	277	3650	765
3.	Bhagamunda	1334	7515	599	4488	2428
4.	Dhurudiamba	910	4884	106	3708	1070
5.	Harichandanpur	1467	7492	499	2435	4558
6.	Sunapentha	1188	5928	449	2779	2700
7.	Rebnapalaspal	1418	7319	169	5404	1746
8.	Junga	878	4481	263	2505	1713
9.	Boxibarigaon	675	3532	331	2520	701
10.	Janghira	1512	7095	391	3683	3021
11.	Jamujodi	1250	6342	835	2217	3290
12.	Hoondapalaspal	921	4826	571	2515	1740
13.	Hoonda	433	4370	423	2342	1605
14.	Pithagola	1291	6465	583	3226	2656
15.	Tentalapasi	1017	5548	136	2396	3016
16.	Manoharpur	1219	6512	716	1854	3942
17.	Bhanapur	859	2968	291	937	1740
18.	Daitary	848	4434	543	1566	2325
	Total	19871	103462	7707	55133	40562

Source : Census of India 1991.

Table 15 : Names of the Villages in the study area of Harichandanpur Block

Sl. No.	Name of the Village	Name of the Panchayat
1.	Baliparbat	Tangiriapal
2.	Barigaon	–do–
3.	Arjunchuan	–do–
4.	Sagadapeta	Sagadapeta
5.	Billa	–do–
6.	Bhagamunda	Bhagamunda
7.	Nuagaon	–do–
8.	Dhurudiamba	Dhurudiamba
9.	Jamuda	–do–
10.	Karadapal	–do–
11.	Haridagotha	Harichandanpur
12.	Raidiha	–do–
13.	Badsialimal	Sunapentha
14.	Kantla	–do–
15.	Rebnapalaspal	Rebnapalaspal
16.	Bangurusuni	–do–
17.	Balaniposi	Junga
18.	Boxibarigaon	Boxibarigaon
19.	Ostapanga	–do–
20.	Janghira	Janghira
21.	Budhakhaman	–do–
22.	Kalapata	Jamujodi
23.	Gargadbahal	Hoondapalaspal
24.	Bhuka	–do–
25.	Hoonda	Hoonda

Source : Listing from B.D.O./ Gram Panchayat Office, Harichandanpur Block.

Table 16 : Names of the Selected Villages, Total Population (SC, ST, & OBC), Harichandanpur Block, District Keonjhar

Sl. No.	Selected Villages	Population				Percentage of ST Population to the Total Population
		Total	SC	ST	OBC	
1.	Baliparbat	1546	192	771	583	49.87
2.	Barigaon	924	35	760	129	82.25
3.	Arjunchuan	891	0	879	12	98.65
4.	Sagadpata	1930	117	1388	425	71.91
5.	Billa	1539	49	1224	266	79.53
6.	Bhagamunda	3559	160	2213	1186	62.18
7.	Nuagaon	924	105	757	62	81.92
8.	Dhunudiamba	1130	3	990	137	87.61
9.	Jamuda	1187	49	937	201	78.93
10.	Karadapal	1232	20	946	266	76.8
11.	Haridagotha	694	2	687	05	98.99
12.	Raidiha	1483	68	740	675	49.89
13.	Badasialimal	1516	63	654	799	43.13
14.	Kantala	1404	206	604	594	43.01
15.	Rebnapalaspal	1520	107	1158	255	76.18
16.	Bangurasuni	792	20	645	127	81.43
17.	Balaniposi	1029	0	791	238	76.80
18.	Boxiburigaon	1260	219	538	503	42.69
19.	Ostapamga	811	9	752	50	92.72
20.	Janghira	1711	214	683	814	39.91
21.	Budhakhaman	1055	0	942	113	89.28
22.	Kalapata	788	81	509	198	64.59
23.	Garagadabahi	986	159	726	101	73.63
24.	Bhuka	731	10	563	158	77.01
25	Hoonda	2403	398	1285	720	53.54
	Total	33045	2286	22142	8617	67.00

Source : Census of India, 1991.

Table 17 : Name of the Gram Panchayats and their Sarpanch

Sl. No.	Name of the Gram Panchayat	Name of the Sarpanch	Sex	Caste
1.	Tangiripal	Biswanath Majhi	M	ST
2.	Sagadapeta	Trilochan Dehuri	M	ST
3.	Bagamunda	Smt. Golap Dehuri	F	ST
4.	Dhurudiamba	Biswakarmi Munda	F	ST
5.	Harichandanpur	Pramod Kr. Sahoo	M	Gen.
6.	Sunapentha	Purnachandra Mohanta	M	Gen.
7.	Rebanapalaspal	Bijoy Kr. Majhi	M	ST
8.	Junga	Bhabagrahi Naik	M	ST
9.	Boxibarigaon	Agasti Naik	M	ST
10.	Janghira	Indumati Das	F	ST
11.	Jamujodi	Minati Sethi	F	SC
12.	Hoondapalaspal	Chandrasekhar Baliarsing	M	ST
13.	Hoonda	Dileswari Amaratiya	F	ST
14.	Pithagola	Nirakar Sahoo	M	Gen.
15.	Tentalapasi	Kanta Behera	F	Gen.
16.	Manoharpur	Dushasana Palei	M	ST
17.	Bhanarpur	Manoj Bej	M	Gen.
18.	Diatary	Chandrasekhar Champia	M	ST

Source : Obtained from BDO/ Gram Panchayat Office of the Harichandanpur Block.

Table 18 : Attendance in Gram Sabha Meetings

Sl. No.	Name of the Gram Panchayat	1997		1998		1999		
		Feb.	June	Feb.	June	Feb.	June	Oct.
1.	Tangiripal	—	45	128	—	160	—	320
2.	Sagadapeta	—	60	185	—	225	60	240
3.	Bagamunda	—	80	220	—	285	90	260
4.	Dhurudiamba	—	—	80	—	75	—	30
5.	Harichandanpur	—	75	120	135	280	180	350
6.	Sunapentha	—	—	65	35	160	40	150
7.	Rebanapalaspal	—	—	30	—	75	—	80
8.	Junga	—	40	85	—	130	50	175
9.	Boxibarigaon	—	60	80	—	180	60	220
10.	Janghira	—	75	125	—	190	75	210
11.	Jamujodi	—	35	75	—	60	30	80
12.	Hoondapalaspal	—	45	60	—	75	—	135
13.	Hoonda	—	60	130	—	60	—	120

Source : Obtained form BDO/Gram Panchayat Office.

Table 19 : Gram Panchayat-wise problems & prospects of selected Gram Panchayats of Harichandanpur Block

Sl. No.	Name of the Gram Panchayat	Major Problems	Prospects of the Area
1.	Tangiripal	1. No link roads 2. Good educational facilities not available 3. Drinking water problem 4. In some parts hygiene is not so good	1. Dense forest 2. MFP processing unit 3. Collection center 4. Dairy development
2.	Sagadapeta	1. Health problems 2. Lack of transport facilities 3. No irrigation facilities 4. Unavailability of jobs for local villagers	1. Reservoir at Billa 2. M.I. at Palabani 3. Dairy development 4. MP Collection centre at Sagadapeta
3.	Bagamunda	1. Kuchha roads from one village to another 2. Marketing of agricultural products 3. No good opportunities for daily labourers 4. Electrification is not done in all the villages	1. Gaunighasha MIP was destroyed in the last Oct. 29th flood. It has to be restored 2. Rain cement culvert (RCC) at Nuagaon 3. Chilikdhara MIP 4. MFP processing unit
4.	Dhurudiamba	1. No link roads 2. No irrigation facilities 3. Marketing of forest products 4. No work in the hands of tribal community 5. Health problems	1. MIP–Chaurimela 2. MFP processing unit at Dhurudiamba 3. RCC/MIP at Karadapal
5.	Harichandanpur	1. Unemployment 2. Shortage of drinking water	1. RCC at Gandadiha 2. MFP–processing unit 3. MIP–Singhbilla 4. Training centre for unemployed youth 5. MFP processing unit Research Centre
6.	Sunapentha	1. No education facilities 2. No link roads 3. No irrigation 4. No work for tribal community	1. MFP processing unit 2. MIP Sunapentha 3. Dairy farm 4. Dense forest

(Contd.)

Table 19 : *(Contd.)*

Sl. No.	Name of the Gram Panchayat	Major Problems	Prospects of the Area
		5. Improper health and hygiene	
7.	Rebanapalaspal	1. No link roads 2. Health problems 3. Shortage of drinking water 4. Malnutrition	1. MFP processing unit 2. MFP collection centre 3. MIP 4. Dairy development 5. Bee-keeping
8.	Junga	1. Health problems 2. No education facilities 3. No link roads 4. Unavailability of work for daily labourers	1. MIP at Junga 2. RCC 3. Dairy development 4. Pig farm 5. MFP–collection centre
9.	Boxibarigaon	1. Marketing for agricultural products 2. Employment problems 3. Health problems 4. No link roads	1. MFP processing unit Training centre 2. Dairy development 3. Health centre 4. MIP
10.	Janghira	1. No link roads 2. Health problems 3. Marketing of forest products	1. MIP at Nadam, Sompur 2. Dairy development
11.	Jamujodi	1. Shortage of drinking water 2. Health problems 3. Education facilities not available	1. Dairy development 2. MFP processing unit 3. Training centre
12.	Hoondapalaspal	1. No link roads 2. No work in the hands of tribals 3. Marketing of forest products	1. MIP–Nula 2. MFP collection centre 3. MFP processing unit 4. Dairy development
13.	Hoonda	1. No link roads 2. Marketing of forest products 3. Unavailability of good education facilities for tribal children 4. Health problems	1. MIP 2. MFP collection centre 3. Dairy development 4. Bee-keeping

Source : Obtained after discussion with BDO/WEOs of Gram Panchayats of Harichandanpur Block.

Table 20 : Problems on Priority Basis

Sl. No.	Name of the Gram Panchayat	Employ-ment	Drink-ing Water	Link Roads	Marketing of Agricul-tural Products, MFP, etc.	Educa-tion	Health	Stopping Exploita-tion
1.	Tangiripal	5	4	1	6	2	3	7
2.	Sagadapeta	6	5	3	4	2	1	7
3.	Begamunda	6	5	1	2	3	4	7
4.	Dhurudiamba	4	3	1	2	7	5	6
5.	Harichandanpur	1	2	5	4	7	3	6
6.	Sunapentha	5	2	2	6	1	4	7
7.	Rebanapalaspal	6	3	1	4	5	2	7
8.	Junga	5	6	4	3	2	1	7
9.	Boxibarigaon	2	6	5	1	3	4	7
10.	Janghira	6	5	2	1	3	4	7
11.	Jamujodi	2	1	2	5	3	6	7
12.	Hoondapalaspal	3	3	1	4	7	6	5
13.	Hoonda	4	3	1	2	6	5	7

Source : Obtained after discussion with the members of Gram Panchayats, BDO/WEOs of Harichandanpur Block.

RAJASTHAN

Introduction

The provisions of the Panchayats (Extension to the Scheduled Areas) Act, 1996 (hereafter referred to as Extension Act) came into force w.e.f. December 24, 1996. It envisages that the concerned State Government should legislate appropriate laws in consonance with the Extension Act in order to, *interalia* transfer powers over enforcement of prohibition, ownership of minor forest produce, land management, village markets etc., to the Gram Sabha or Panchayats at appropriate level in the Scheduled Areas. Besides, the Extension Act stipulates that the traditions and culture of the people of the Scheduled Areas, should be honoured and fully protected. The State legislatures of the Fifth Schedule Areas comprising the eight States are thus required to amend their existing Panchayat Acts and other laws to be in consonance with the provisions of the Extension Act within the stipulated time period of one year from its enactment i.e. by 23rd December, 1997. But, none of the concerned States enacted their Acts in conformity with the Extension Act till August 1997. Consequently, in order to hasten the process of implementation of the Extension Act, the then Ministry of Rural Areas and Employment organised a meeting of the State Ministers of Panchayati Raj and Tribal Welfare on 8.9.1997 at New Delhi. At the meeting, the Secretary (Panchayati Raj), Rajasthan mentioned "...there is no need of this Act in Rajasthan. There is no resentment or discontent among the tribals of Rajasthan. Rajasthan Panchayati Raj Act, 1994, therefore, does not need any changes ....the reservation for Scheduled Tribes according to the population has already been made in the Rajasthan Panchayati Raj Act.... We should wait for another 2-3 years before giving more powers to Gram Sabha." This, to an extent, shows the mind set of the then government in power about giving authority to the tribal people who had not been protected against policies which went against them due to their vulnerability. In a nutshell, the conformity legislation could not be amended in consonance with the Extension Act till the deadline i.e. 23rd

December 1997. In the meantime, a new government led by Ashok Ghalot was voted to power in the State. The new government took initiatives to extend the provisions of the Extension Act in the Scheduled Areas. For the purpose, the State Government conducted a number of seminars and workshops on the subject. Finally, the State Government issued an Ordinance namely, the 'Rajasthan Panchayati Raj (Modification of Provisions in their Application to the Scheduled Areas) Ordinance, 1999' to implement the Extension Act in the Scheduled Areas of the State. This Rajasthan Ordinance was replaced by an Act in June, 1999. Accordingly, elections to Panchayats were held according to the new Act in January, 2000. A large number of Scheduled Tribe members were elected by various levels of Panchayats. Details of ST members elected are not readily available.

Area of Operation of the Act in the State

In Rajasthan, the Scheduled Areas have been specified *vide* the Presidential order dated December 7, 1950, subsequently modified vide Notification No. F. 19 (2)/ 80-L-3, dated 12.2.1981. The redefined Scheduled Areas comprise: Banswara district, Dungarpur district, entire tehsils of Phalasia, Kherwara, Katra, Sarada, Salumber and Lasadia and 81 villages of Girwa tehsil of Udaipur district, Pratapgarh tehsil in Chittorgarh district and Abu road block of Abu road tehsil in Sirohi district. This area is co-terminus with the Tribal-Sub Plan (TSP) area.

Appraisal of the Rajasthan Panchayati Raj (Modification of Provisions in their Application to the Scheduled Areas) Ordinance, 1999

The Ordinance contains provisions of the Extension Act from Section 4 (a) to (h), except clearly identifying which tier of the Panchayat would perform which specified function i.e. *instead of clearly demarcating the functions either at Gram Sabha level or at the level of any tier of the Panchayati Raj Institutions (PRIs), it states Gram Sabha or PRIs thus opening multi-options and ambiguity.*

With regard to Section 4 (i) to (l) of the Extension Act, instead of specification of functions and powers clearly, phrases such as "may be prescribed" or "in such manner as may be prescribed" have been used by the State Government.

Besides, Section 4 (m) of the Extension Act specifies that while endowing Panchayats in the Scheduled Areas with such powers and authority as may be necessary to enable them to function as institutions of self-government, the State legislature shall ensure that the Panchayat at the appropriate level and the Gram Sabha are endowed specifically with the powers to enforce prohibition, sale and consumption of any intoxicant, ownership of minor forest produce, prevent alienation of land, management of village markets, control over money-lending, exercise control over institutions and functionaries in all social sectors and control over local plans and resources for such plans including Tribal Sub-Plan.

The Conformity Ordinance instead of giving these powers to the Panchayats and Grama Sabha, mentioned that "The Panchayati Raj Institutions at appropriate level or Grama Sabha as may be prescribed, in a Scheduled Area". It implies that Grama Sabha and Panchayats would not be constituted compulsorily as mentioned in the Extension Act. Further phrases, such as "in the manner to be specified by the State Government from time to time" are either prefixed or suffixed almost to all provisions of the Ordinance relating to above mentioned functions.

Further, provisions have not been made in the Ordinance in the light of Section 4 (n) and (o) of the Extension Act, which are very important from the point of view of making Panchayats in Scheduled Areas as institutions of self-government in order to provide autonomy to the Panchayats as well as Gram Sabha and allow the State legislature to endeavour to follow the pattern of the Sixth Schedule to the Constitution atleast at district level.

In brief the Ordinance does not incorporate either in letter or spirit the contents of the Extension Act.

In connection with the promulgation of the Ordinance, it is significant that the M.L. Verma Tribal Research and Training Institute, Udaipur, had conducted two Workshops during mid-1998 (30-31 July) and the beginning of 1999 (20-21 Feb). In these workshops elected representatives, social workers, bureaucrats and intellectuals participated and brought out the following aspects for consideration of the State Government while enacting the conformity legislation in consonance with the Extension Act.

(1) The size of population of the Gram Sabha might be between 200 and 300. To make Gram Sabha's meeting a practical exercise existing ward may be designated as Gram Sabha.
(2) About the customs and traditions, cultural identities and customary mode of dispute resolution, it was suggested that traditions and customs relating to marriage, property quarrel (simple nature) protection and use of community resources and cooperative life encompassing voluntary labour, exchange 'Natra' and 'Potali' etc. should be codified.
(3) Fifty per cent share of women should constitute the quorum of Gram Sabha.
(4) Appealing agency on the decisions taken by the Gram Sabha in social matters should be the Panchayat Samiti Development Officer; on economic matters, Zilla Parishad Administrative Officer and jurisdiction of court and the police could be decided after taking into consideration the findings of the Panchayat Samiti Development Officer.
(5) If a particular plan or activity relates to more than one Gram Sabha then the appropriate level should be either Panchayat Samiti or Zilla Parishad. In addition, functions to be performed by each tier of the Panchayati Raj Institution and Gram Sabha should be identified.

The Ordinance does not reflect the views expressed in the workshops. These were relevant for amendment of the State Panchayat Act. It is hoped that the Rules and Procedures to be laid down might contain explicit provisions regarding powers and functions of the Panchayats.

The field study

It may be recalled that the elections to the Panchayats in Rajasthan including the Scheduled Areas were held in 1995 in accordance with the earlier Panchayat Act. The Extension Act has not been opreationalised so far. The State Government has not done any detailed exercise like formulating rules and amending different laws and regulations, having bearing on the Extension Act. It was gathered from discussions at the Tribal Commissioner's Office that the Act would be implemented after the next elections, to be held in January 2000. However, after visiting some Gram Panchayats, Panchayat Samitis discussion with some NGOs, particularly 'Seva Mandir' and 'Astha Block Officials', Tribal Commissioner, Tribal Research and Training Institute, MLAs, and knowledgeable people, following facts on implementation of the Extension Act emerged.

(1) The officials were aware that there is a separate Act for the Fifth Schedule Areas passed by the Parliament in 1996 keeping in view the recommendations of the Bhuria Committee. Also, in consonance with the same, an Ordinance was promulgated by the Rajasthan Government in June 1999. They were aware that more powers have been given to the Gram Sabha on control and preservation of land, water and forest. But they were not aware as to how it would be implemented. They also asked if the Gram Sabha is empowered to perform all major functions affecting tribal economy what would be the role of Sarpanch (President of Gram Panchayat) at Gram Panchayat level and members and chairpersons of higher tiers of the Panchayats. They raised certain issues regarding dispute resolution and customary practices such as, 'Nata' etc. which were not appreciated even by the educated persons among tribals. In fact, educated tribals were mainstreaming themselves by leaving their traditional customs and traditions.

When Jhadol Panchayat Samiti's Officials were asked about the awareness generation and imparting training to the elected representatives about new Panchayati Raj System, they showed helplessness on account of lack of funds for such activities.

(2) Wherever NGOs have been working on issues affecting tribals' life in addition to Panchayati Raj, there was awareness among villagers about self-rule ordained by Extension Act. Some of it were noticed at local level, for example, 'Astha' Voluntary Organisation which is concentrating on this issue particularly in Dungarpur and Banswara districts and some villages of Kotra tehsil of Udaipur district has installed around 40 pillars inscribing on them the functions of the Gram Sabha. This had a tremendous positive impact on villagers. In some villages, Gram Sabha refused the contractors to take away Date's leaves arguing that now onwards it was the property of the Gram Sabha, which would take decisions about its disposal or use. Besides, in some villages, people instead of going to Police Station for lodging complaints are reported to have sorted out minor disputes on their own. It is also found that teachers' attendance in schools has increased and they have also started to be punctual after Gram Sabha vigil.

(3) It is interesting to note that due to awareness about Gram Sabha, the non-scheduled areas were also affected positively, in those villages where NGOs were working on the issue and tribals have also been actively participating as voluntary workers. In this context, one such example of Bagdunda Khare of Gogunda tehsil of district Udaipur is worth mentioning. In the village, a pillar was erected on June 21, 1999, inscribing on it the powers and functions of the Gram Sabha listed in the Extension Act even before the Ordinance was passed by the State Government. This exercise sensitised the tribal people about the title on ownership of their land, forest and water and provided an opportunity to solve their problems by themselves. In another case of dispute over land between two families, the issue was sorted out by the Gram Sabha itself. It happened after both the disputing parties lodged a complain in the police station, and were advised by the officer in-charge that they themselves can resolve the issue keeping in view their traditions and customs as self-rule has been established in their village.

The parties thereafter settled the issue amicably.

In yet another case of dispute between father and son over land, as usual, they also went to the police station. The police station in-charge again gave them the same advice and the issue was settled by the elders of the village. The people of the village were happy on yet another count; their village was electrified after establishing self-rule.

(4) As the post of chairperson of all tiers of the Panchayats has been reserved for the Scheduled Tribe, irrespective of their population ratio in the Panchayat, there was dissatisfaction among non-tribals in Rajasthan particularly at the Gram Panchayat level, because they would not have Sarpanchship at any time. In some parts of Banswara district non-tribals have protested against these provisions. It is also feared that the non-tribal people may go to the court and may scuttle the process of implementation of the Extension Act by holding election to the Panchayats which are due in January 2000. But when a tribal who knew about the provision was asked, he said, "what is the harm if the post is reserved for tribals because these upper caste people have been enjoying sarpanchship, pradhanship and presidentship since the inception of Panchayati Raj in these areas". This shows a feeling of self-confidence among tribals who are educated and understand the mechanism of their exploitation over the centuries.

(5) Some Gram Panchayats, like Baleecha in Girwa tehsil of Udaipur district are well developed and have almost become a part of the mainstream. There are a number of Gram Panchayats in the vicinity of Udaipur city, which are well-developed and are entirely different from the rest of the villages of Girwa and other villages of Fifth Schedule Areas of the district. Above mentioned Baleecha village is situated about 5-6 km from Udaipur city on the Ahmedabad highway. There is one petrol pump, a number of hotels and Dhabas, clinics and repair shops in the village. When asked, the Sarpanch who happened to be a woman, as to why tax has not been imposed on these activities for enhancing own resources of the

Panchayat, she did not say anything.

(6) Shri Khem Raj Katra, MLA (Bhil Tribe) was not in favour of continuing the TSP strategy and having separate administrative structure for tribal development. He termed TSP strategy as "empty box" containing nothing while consuming scarce resources of the government through creating separate bureaucratic infrastructure for nothing. He expressed similar views on Tribal Cooperative Federation and said unless and until these institutions are governed/managed by tribal people themselves, they are not going to benefit the tribals. He said that the plans should be prepared from below and that the entire plan resources should be placed in the hands of the tribals.

To conclude, the purpose of the Extension Act has not been understood entirely, neither by the political leadership nor by the bureaucracy. People at large are not aware about the latest system of tribal self-rule except in those areas where NGOs were working with the people, and where tribal people were also working in these NGOs as social activists. *There are a number of State laws relating to money-lending, forest, excise etc. which have to be amended in the light of the Extension Act and State Panchayat Acts.* The entire picture of the implementation of the Extension Act would be clear after the next election of the Panchayats which are scheduled to be held in the month of January 2000*.

---

* Elections were held, as scheduled.

3

A Critical Analysis of the Provisions of Panchayats (Extension to Scheduled Areas) Act, 1996 and Implementation

Article 243M of the Constitution provides that "nothing in this Part* shall apply to the Scheduled Areas referred to in Clause (1), and the Tribal Areas referred to in Clause (2) of Article 244". But, according to Article 243M 4 (b), it is provided that 'Parliament may, by law extend provisions of this Part to the Scheduled Areas and Tribal Areas referred to in Clause (1), subject to such exceptions and modifications as may be specified in such law'. In most of the States, having Scheduled Areas, Panchayat elections were either held uniformly with other areas as in Madhya Pradesh (1994) and Rajasthan (1995) or results withheld after the elections like in Andhra Pradesh. The extension of the 73rd Constitution Amendment Act (hereafter called Central Act) in the Scheduled Areas was challenged in the High Courts of Andhra Pradesh, Orissa and Maharashtra and the matter was stayed for the time being.

The extension was viewed as ultra-vires to the Constitution by the courts and held that the Central Act could be extended to the Scheduled Areas only through an Act of Parliament. Consequently, to look into these matters, a Committee under the Chairmanship of Dileep Singh Bhuria was constituted in June 1994. The Committee consisted of 22 members, of whom 15 were Members of Parliament

---

* Part IX - Panchayats.

(including the Chairman) and others included experts and serving officers in the Government of India.

The Committee submitted its report in January, 1995. It *interalia* dealt with the issues of participatory democracy, effectiveness of customary laws, community control over resources and appropriate administrative framework for the Scheduled Areas. The Committee felt that while sharing the new Panchayati Raj structure in tribal areas, it is desirable to blend the traditional with the modern by treating the traditional institutions as the foundation on which the modern super structure should be built and taking cognizance of their indigenous institutions and ethos while considering democratic decentralization in tribal areas.

The following are some of the major recommendations of the Bhuria Committee.

Structure

(1) The Committee recommended a three-tier Panchayat structure at the village level, intermediate and district level which resembled the provisions of Part IX of the Constitution. Recommendations regarding powers were quite elaborate and that the powers to be given to Panchayats in Scheduled Areas should aim at combating and preventing the exploitation of tribals and building up the political, economic and social strength of the tribal communities. These Panchayati Raj Institutions (PRIs) should also be vested with adequate powers to deal with emerging problems among tribal people, like growing indebtedness, land alienation, de-forestation, ecological degradation, displacement, excise policy, water resources etc. Further, these powers should emanate from the Constitution and not left to the discretion of the States. The recommendation of the Committee with regard to powers and functions of the Gram Sabhas, Gram Panchayats, Intermediate Panchayats and the autonomous district council were comprehensively spelt out.

The Government took some time to enact the Bill after the Bhuria Committee made its recommendations and this delay was resented, as witnessed in protest demonstrations by various non-governmental organizations and social groups, with the National Front for Tribal Self-rule in the lead. There was also an indefinite fast undertaken by 32 tribal representatives from all over the country at Rajghat in Delhi on February 16, 1996. The fast was broken on the 10th day after an assurance by the then Minister of Parliamentary Affairs. But as the assurance was not met, a large number of tribal representatives from all over the country organized intensive campaign and agitational programmes in Delhi during September 2-6, 1996. Finally, the Act known as the "Provisions of the Panchayats (Extension to the Scheduled Areas) Act, 1996" came into force on 24th December 1996. (Annexure-II)

In brief, the entire focus of the Bhuria Committee Report was to establish participative democracy in conformity with the customary laws, social practices and traditional management of common resources.

Distinctive features of the Provisions of the Panchayats (Extension to the Scheduled Areas) Act, 1996

The provisions of the Panchayats (Extension to the Scheduled Area) Act, 1996, extends to the Panchayats in the Fifth Schedule Areas of eight States viz. Andhra Pradesh, Bihar, Gujarat, Himachal Pradesh, Maharashtra, Madhya Pradesh, Orissa and Rajasthan. Following are the major features of the Extension Act.

(i) Any legislation on the Panchayats for Vth Schedule Area shall be in agreement with the customary law, social and religious practices and traditional management practice of the community resources of its inhabitants.

(ii) Powers vested in Gram Sabha for: (a) Ownership of minor forest produce, (b) Approval of development plans, (c) Selection of beneficiaries under various programmes, (d) Consultation on land acquisition, (e) Management of minor water bodies, (f) Control of minor minerals, (g) Regulation of prohibition of sale of intoxicants, (h) Prevention of alienation of land and restoration of unlawfully alienated land of STs, (i) Management of village markets, (j) Control of money lending to STs (k) Controlling institutions and functionaries in all social sectors, (l) Giving utilisation certificate for funds used for the projects and programmes of social and economic development etc. to the village Panchayats.

(iii) Reservation of seats for the Scheduled Tribes at all tiers of the Panchayats shall not be less than half of the total number of seats. Reservation for other communities indicated in Part IX of the Constitution shall be in proportion to the population of such communities.

(iv) The Chairpersonship at all levels of the Panchayats shall be reserved for the STs.

(v) In case the STs do not have representation at intermediate or apex level of Panchayati Raj System, the State Government shall nominate such unrepresented Scheduled Tribes, but such nomination should not exceed one-tenth of the total elected members of the Panchayats.

The State legislatures should take into consideration the following aspects while amending their respective Panchayat Acts.

(a) Gram Sabha should be made head and heart of entire scheme of decentralisation by way of according independence in managing, protecting and preserving natural resources and formulation of plans, projects and schemes for holistic development of tribal people.

(b) Panchayats should take approval of the Gram Sabha in all matters effecting tribal economy and society. In other words, relationship between the Gram Sabha and the Panchayat should be similar to the one existing between legislatures and the government.

(c) The underlying spirit of the Extension Act is on devolution instead of giving powers and authority to the Gram Sabha. It represents participatory democracy rather than empowering representative decentralised democracy.

(d) While devolving powers and authority on Panchayat or Gram Sabha, State legislatures should ensure that Panchayats at higher level do not assume the powers and authority of any Panchayat at lower level or of the Gram Sabha.

A comparison between the Extension Act and conformity legislations. The State-wise comparison of conformity legislations with the Extension Act has been given in Annexure III.

It is generally assumed that the tribal societies are homogeneous and monolithic and also have cultural and traditional methods to work together in a participatory manner. Thus decentralised democracy in the form of the Gram Sabha is appropriate for them. Bhuria Committee recommended that the Gram Sabha be made the cornerstone of entire decentralised governance, planning and development.

Legislatures of the States with Fifth Schedule Areas were required to amend their respective Panchayat Acts in conformity with the Extension Act before the expiry of one year of the Extension Act coming into force, i.e. 23rd December 1997. All the States except Bihar amended their Acts. The Rajasthan Government promulgated an Ordinance on June 30th, 1999 to implement the provisions of the Extension Act, later replaced by an Act.

Traditional Rights of Tribals

In Gujarat, Himachal Pradesh, Rajasthan and Madhya Pradesh, State Panchayat Acts have empowered the Gram Sabha to safeguard and preserve the traditions and customs of the people, their cultural identity, community resources and the customary mode of dispute resolution in conformity with the Extension Act. Andhra Pradesh, Maharashtra and Orissa Panchayat Acts have qualified these powers with the provisions, such as without detriment to any law for the time being in force, and consistent with "relevant law in force and in harmony with the tenets of the Constitution and human rights" respectively.

Approval of Plans, Programmes and Projects by the Gram Sabha

Extension Act has empowered the Gram Sabha to approve plans, programmes and projects as well as identify beneficiaries and issue utilisation certificate of funds. *All conformity legislations have made this provision in their State Panchayat Acts.*

Acquisition of Land

Prior consultation with the Gram Sabha or the Panchayat before acquiring land for development projects and before resettling or rehabilitating the affected persons.

The Andhra Pradesh and Gujarat Panchayat Acts, instead of giving this function to Gram Sabha, have assigned it to the Mandal Panchayat and Taluka Panchayat (Intermediate tier) respectively. Orissa Panchayat Act has given this function to the Zilla Panchayat. Himachal Pradesh and Maharashtra Act have given this task to the Gram Sabha. Madhya Pradesh Act does not specify it in clear terms except saying that the Gram Sabha will manage natural resources including land. The Rajasthan Ordinance has given this power to the Gram Sabha or Panchayati Raj Institutions as may be prescribed. Hence, no uniform pattern emerges from the provisions of the State Panchayat Acts. This might be due to the provision contained in the Extension Act itself, which has given option to States to devolve power either to the Gram Sabha or the Panchayat (Panchayat may be at lowest level or at intermediate level or at apex level). However, *Himachal Pradesh and Maharashtra have reasonably kept the spirit of the Extension Act.*

Management of Minor Water Bodies

Planning and management of minor water bodies was to be entrusted to the Panchayats at the appropriate level. The Andhra Pradesh Panchayat Act has made provision for giving this function to any tier of the Panchayati Raj System. Himachal Pradesh has followed Andhra Pradesh without specifying which tier shall bear this responsibility. Such provisions create confusion, i.e. the absence of clear cut demarcation of function. Gujarat Panchayat Act has assigned this responsibility to the Taluka Panchayat and Orissa Panchayat Act has given it to the apex tier of the Panchayat. Maharashtra Panchayati Raj Act has ignored this function and has not made any provision. In Rajasthan, this responsibility has been given to Panchayats as may be specified by the State Government. Madhya Pradesh Panchayat Act has made provision that the Gram Panchayat would take advise of the Gram Sabha in planning and management of the minor water bodies.

Minor Minerals

As per the Extension Act, prior recommendation by the Gram Sabha or by the Panchayat at appropriate level is required for granting of prospecting licence or mining lease for minor minerals in the Scheduled Area and granting concession for the exploitation of minor minerals by auction, but no uniform pattern has emerged across the States. This might be due to the provision contained in Extension Act itself in which provision for the Gram Sabha or the Gram Panchayat is made. Andhra Pradesh, Gujarat and Maharashtra Panchayat Acts (for granting concession) have given these powers to the Gram Panchayat whereas Himachal Pradesh awarded this function to Gram Sabha. The Orissa Panchayat Act has given this power to the Zilla Parishad whereas Madhya Pradesh has not made any mention in this regard. Maharashtra Panchayat Act has made provision for every Panchayat, without specifying which tier would be assigned what aspect of this function. Rajasthan has made provision for the Gram Sabha or PRIs in such manner as may be prescribed.

Powers of the Panchayat and the Gram Sabha

The Extension Act specifies that while endowing Panchayats in the Scheduled Area with such powers and authority as may be necessary to enable them to function as institutions of self-government, the State legislature shall ensure that the Panchayat at the appropriate level and the Gram Sabha are endowed specifically with :

(i) Power to enforce prohibition or regulation in respect of sale and consumption of any intoxicant. (ii) Ownership of minor forest produce. (iii) Prevention of alienation of land in the Scheduled Areas and powers to take appropriate action to restore any unlawfully alienated land of STs. (iv) Powers to manage village markets. (v) Provisions of money-lending to the STs. (vi) Exercising control over institutions and functionaries in all social sectors. (vii) Control over local plans and resources.

Power to Enforce Prohibition

State Panchayat Acts of Andhra Pradesh and Himachal Pradesh have given this function to the Gram Sabha or the Gram Panchayat as the case may be, while the Gujarat Panchayat Act has given it to the intermediate tier. Maharashtra and Orissa Panchayat Acts have given this task to the Gram Sabha whereas Madhya Pradesh Panchayat Act does not mention anything about this. Rajasthan Ordinance made provisions for PRI and Gram Sabha, as may be prescribed by the State Government.

Ownership of Minor Forest Produce

State Panchayat Acts of Andhra Pradesh, Himachal Pradesh and Madhya Pradesh have given this power to the Gram Sabha or the Gram Panchayat. Gujarat Panchayat Act has given it to the village Panchayat. Maharashtra and Orissa Panchayat Acts have given this power to the Gram Sabha. In Rajasthan none of the Panchayat tier has been made responsible for this function.

Preventing Alienation of Land

Andhra Pradesh and Himachal Pradesh Panchayat Acts have given this responsibility to the Gram Panchayat or the Gram Sabha. Gujarat and Madhya Pradesh Panchayat Acts have not made any mention about this aspect. Although Maharashtra and Orissa Panchayat Acts have given this function to the Gram Sabha, the latter has specified that the Gram Sabha could make recommendations to the Panchayat. In Rajasthan it is mentioned that appropriate action would be taken up in accordance with the land laws.

Managing Village Markets

State Panchayat Acts of Andhra Pradesh and Madhya Pradesh have given the power to the Gram Sabha or the Gram Panchayat. Orissa Panchayat Act has empowered the Gram Sabha while Gujarat and Maharashtra Panchayat Acts have not specified it. The Rajasthan Ordinance mentions "subject to such rules as may be specified by the State Government".

Control over Institutions and Functionaries

Andhra Pradesh, Gujarat and Himachal Pradesh Panchayat Acts have given this authority to intermediate level of the Panchayat whereas Madhya Pradesh has given it to the Gram Sabha. For social sector, the Maharashtra Panchayat Act has made provision for involving every Panchayat and has given recommendatory power to the Gram Sabha for local plans. Orissa Panchayat Act has given this task to the Panchayat (intermediate tier), but in consultation with the Gram Sabha. The Rajasthan Ordinance prescribed, "to the extent and in manner as may be prescribed".

A comparison across the States reveals that State Panchayat Acts of Maharashtra and Orissa (and to some extent Madhya Pradesh) are alert to the situation as they have devolved such functions to the Gram Sabha, which is invariably in control over these important aspects of tribal village life and economy in a collective manner.

Panchayats as Self-Governing Institutions

The Extension Act has provided that the State may endow

Panchayats with the powers and authority as may be necessary to enable them to function as institutions of self-government. Surprisingly, none of the State legislatures has made any specific provision for making the Panchayat an institution of self-government by providing adequate safeguards so that the Panchayat at higher level does not assume powers and authority of the Panchayats at the lower level and the Gram Sabha. This is a serious omission.

Adoption of Sixth Schedule

According to the Extension Act the State legislation shall endeavour to follow the pattern of the Sixth Schedule of the Constitution while designing the administrative arrangement for the Panchayat at district level.

Adoption of Sixth Schedule Areas arrangement is very important for making panchayats, in real sense, institutions of self-government because under the Sixth Schedule, District Councils perform legislative, judicial and administrative functions in their jurisdiction. It also implies that the administrative machinery dealing with social and non-social sectoral programmes would be put under the control of Panchayats. In a meeting of State Ministers and Secretaries organised by the Ministry of Rural Areas and Employment on 8.9.97, the Secretary, Rural Development had also drawn attention of the State Governments towards this provision while drafting their legislation. But the State Governments have not paid any attention to adopting of the Sixth Schedule Area arrangement for administrative structure and has left out this provision while drafting their Panchayat Acts to be in conformity with the Extension Act.

The following conclusion emerges from the above presentation.

The rationale behind the Extension Act was to empower Gram Sabha to approve and sanction all matters pertaining to tribal society and economy. The role of Panchayats at different levels was merely to execute decisions taken by the Gram Sabha. In this respect State Panchayat Acts of Maharashtra and Himachal Pradesh are in greater consonance with the Extension Act.

In the Extension Act, functions, power and responsibilities have been assigned to either "Gram Sabha and Panchayat" or "Gram Sabha or Panchayat". Thus, one can conclude that a particular function given in the Extension Act has to be first approved by the Gram Sabha and then executed and/or implemented by the Panchayat. In some States, words like "every Panchayat" have been used, which create confusion because it does not specify which tier would perform which function.

The analysis also leads to the conclusion that the provisions of different State Panchayat Acts have largely been influenced by the attitude and approach of the State Government towards understanding and seeking solutions to tribal problems. The views expressed at the meeting of the State Ministers of Panchayati Raj and Tribal Welfare held on 8.9.97 at New Delhi, with the purpose to discuss the progress of the implementation of Extension Act, reflected these preferences and prejudices. It is noteworthy that the then Secretary, Rural Development lamented: "It was unfortunate that certain elements in the bureaucracy still had anti-tribal and anti-poor bias. When it comes to helping the rich, laws and policies are flouted to be implemented". Citing the examples of Orissa and Maharashtra he said that: "In Orissa, control over bamboo forests has been leased out to a private trader, against the Forest Policy and the Forest Conservation Act. In Maharashtra, Ballarpur Paper Mill gets heavily subsidised bamboo which is against the National Forest Policy. In another State 1200 houses of poor innocent tribals were burnt on the ground that they were sympathetic to naxalites. Despite many such atrocities being brought to the notice of State Governments little action is taken." Besides this, he regretted "that the States were recommending postponement of the present legislation knowing fully well that extra time will not lead to additional knowledge on the subject. He appealed to the State Ministers not to accept such recommendations".

Critical Issues

There are certain problems, both with certain Central laws and State legislations passed in pursuance of the Extension Act, 1996.

The crucial issues are:

(a) *Definition of Minor Forest Produce*: The Indian Forest Act, 1927 defines timber as including, within its definition, bamboo as well as cane. The Ministry of Environment and Forests defines Minor Forest Produce to exclude timber. While doing so, they have decided to adopt the definition of timber which includes not only trees but also bamboo and cane. In most States, tribals have been traditionally depending on bamboo and cane for their livelihood. However, over the last so many years, Forest Corporations and Forest Departments have prevented access to tribals to bamboo and cane, while at the same time giving these to private industry at highly concessional rates. In many cases, tribals have been driven to desperation on account of this policy of State Forest Departments. It is felt that the definition of timber in the 1927 Central Act is neither scientific nor equitable. It is a colonial definition and goes against the spirit of the provisions of the Extension Act,1996.

(b) The interpretation by the Ministry of Environment and Forests of the intention of Parliament regarding vesting of ownership of Minor Forest Produce in Gram Sabhas must be resolved. The proposals made by the Ministry of Environment and Forests interpret the intention of Parliament as giving not ownership *per se,* but making available to the Gram Sabhas, residual profits of State Forest Corporations/Federations. This necessarily means that according to the Ministry of Environment and Forests, State Forest Corporations/Federations will continue to trade in Minor Forest Produce and if there is any surplus, that surplus will be given to the Gram Sabhas. The continued application of the Forest Produce Trade Nationalisation Acts of the States of Maharashtra and Gujarat contravene the provision of the Extension Act in that, powers of control over Minor Forest Produce vested in Gram Sabha is curtailed.

The Rural Development Ministry took up these issues with the Ministry of Environment and Forests and Law and Justice. The

Ministry of Law and Justice stated that the definition adopted by the Ministry of Environment and Forest of Minor Forest Produce was not binding. It further observed that the definition given in one Statute was for effectuating the provisions of the Statute and not for effectuating the provisions of another Statute and further, it was dangerous while interpreting one Act to travel beyond the same and apply definitions of other Acts except those of the General Clause Act, 1897. Ministry of Law also pointed out that the Indian Forest Act, 1927 also does not define Minor Forest Produce. It was stated that under this law, there were mainly two elements in the definition of Forest Produce, namely, timber and all the forest produce other than timber. Further, the PSEA Act, 1996 nowhere says that the definition of the term 'Forest Produce' given in the Indian Forest Act, 1927 shall apply to the said Act.

In so far as interpretation of ownership is concerned, the Law Ministry has been unequivocal in its opinion that no Ministry can circumscribe or limit the scope of ownership endowed with the Extension Act.

The Conference of Secretaries of Rural Development and Panchayati Raj held on 3-4 June, 1999 identified the following major issues in the implementation of the Extension Act.

(i) Whether all State Subject Laws have been amended to bring them in consonance with the Extension Act.

(ii) Extension Act is not an additional law, but is in supersession of all existing laws on the subject. Whether this has been brought to the notice of all concerned.

(iii) Are the amended State laws in conformity with the Central Act.

(iv) What have the State Governments done to implement the legislation.

(v) Have the people in Scheduled V Area been informed of the changes in the legislation.

(vi) Have they been made aware of their rights over natural resources.

Hence, relevant Acts of the State Governments need to be amended in order to fully implement the Extension Act.

Conclusion

To conclude, the Extension Act has been one of the important legislative measures of recent times which recognised the tribal people's mode of living, their culture and traditions. Unfortunately, most of the States have not shown enough zeal and enthusiasm in translating this legislation into practice by making required provisions in their respective Panchayat Acts. The satisfying aspect is that a beginning has been made. There are reservations and hurdles in implementing the Act in its entirety, which are being now debated. It is hoped that in the near future, the provisions of the Central and conformity legislations would enable the tribal people to have access to basic livelihood resources and lead a life without exploitation but with honour and dignity. The one summary conclusion that has emerged from the study is that 'hesitancy' and 'bias' in dealing with the poor but deserving, have to be tackled effectively in the development culture, if Constitutional obligations are to be fulfilled. This view is substantiated by the recent decision of the Government of India to appoint a Constitution "Review Committee".

4

Conclusions and Recommendations

The Report in four chapters (with annexures, tables and maps) follows a sequence. We took this opportunity to refer to the general aspects of tribal development as well because it was felt that at the grass-roots level, the functioning of the Gram Sabha or the Village Panchayat will have manifestations of the system prevailing at that level. Various official documents have directly or indirectly described the discontent and unrest prevailing in some parts of the Scheduled and Tribal Areas. This calls for constant vigil, remedial measures and responsive administration with tribal people's effective participation.

The incorporation of provisions in Part IX of the Constitution relating to Panchayats pursuant to the 73rd Constitutional Amendment Act is an epoch making event in the democratic governance of our country. In particular, Article 243(M) reflects the understanding of the law makers and commitment of the nation in dealing with the population groups like the Scheduled Tribes and undeveloped areas like Fifth Schedule Areas. The report of the Bhuria Committee and enactment of Panchayats (Extension to Scheduled Areas) Act, 1996 are aimed at strengthening the Constitutional and legal safeguard package for the protection and promotion of the interests of the Scheduled Tribes and raising the level of the administration in the Scheduled Areas and translating into action the concept of participatory democracy.

With the exception of Bihar, all the States having Scheduled Areas (Andhra Pradesh, Gujarat, Himachal Pradesh, Madhya Pradesh, Maharashtra, Orissa and Rajasthan) have brought into force the conformity legislations to give effect to the provisions in the Extension Act, 1996. Chapter-3 of the report analyses in detail, the shortcomings noticed in the conformity legislation of individual States. In general, the States have shown wisdom and initiative to provide to the Scheduled Areas the essentials of participatory democracy. These provisions should be improved for which there exist ample scope.

The field studies in Maharashtra and Orissa, and to a limited extent in Rajasthan, have revealed that all is not well with the implementation of the Extension Act. There is need to amend the legislations and re-define planning and implementation strategies.

The first recommendation that we would like to place before the Ministry of Tribal Affairs for consideration, amply substantiated by field situation and analysis of the concerned Acts, would be that a High Level Committee should be appointed, to report within a period of say, six months, the status of implementation of the Extension Act and conformity legislations in all the Fifth Schedule Area States. Further, a Coordination Committee consisting of among others, the nominees of Ministries of Tribal Affairs, Rural Development (incharge of Panchayats), Planning Commission and the Finance Ministry may be constituted to monitor the implementation of the provisions of the Act (both Central and States) in the Scheduled Areas, State by State. Thereafter, the Ministry of Tribal Affairs may make a situational analysis and decide the future course of action to implement the provision of the Extension Act effectively.

Other recommendations are:

1. The one summary conclusion that has emerged from the study is that 'hesitancy' and 'bias' in dealing with the poor but deserving have to be tackled effectively in the development culture, if Constitutional obligations are to be fulfilled. This view is substantiated by the recent decision of the Government of India to appoint a Constitution "Review Committee".
2. The rationale behind Extension Act was to empower Gram Sabha to approve and sanction all matters pertaining to tribal

society and economy. The role of Panchayats at different levels would be merely to execute decisions taken by the Gram Sabha. In this respect State Panchayat Acts of Maharashtra and Himachal Pradesh are in greater consonance with the Extension Act than others.

3. The interpretation regarding vesting of ownership of Minor Forest Produce in Gram Sabha must be resolved.
4. The State Governments should re-examine the issue of adopting the Sixth Schedule Area arrangement for administrative structure to be in conformity with the Extension Act.
5. As none of the State Acts contain any specific provision for making the Panchayat an institution of self-government by providing adequate safeguards so that the Panchayat at higher level does not assume powers and authority of the Panchayats at the lower level and the Gram Sabha, the States must consider the matter.
6. The State laws relating to money-lending, forest, excise etc. have to be amended in the light of the provisions in the Extension Act.
7. Coordination should be ensured in the activities of the TDCC/ ITDA/ ITDP/ Block/financial institutions and the Panchayats to ensure harmonious and balanced utilisation of resources (men, money and material) for achieving plans/ programmes/ project targets.
8. The analysis of gathered data indicates that the major problems faced by the Gram Panchayats are related to insufficiency of drinking water, electrification of hamlets, lack of internal roads as well as link roads and lack of transport facilities, inadequate health and educational facilities, drainage system, absence of functional office space, veterinary dispensary and public latrines, soil conservation and measures for land development. These basic needs must be given priority in planning.
9. The Gram Sabha, should function as a guiding organisation in the Scheduled Areas and their recommendations must be made mandatory on the Gram Panchayats.
10. The customary laws, focussing on good administration and principles of co-existence should be codified.

11. Training and sensitisation programmes for elected Panchayat representatives and functionaries must receive utmost attention.
12. A rapid survey of such heterogeneous tribal groups in a village Panchayat must be made by the district administration to chalk out plausible strategies for development.
13. Those development projects, which cover more than one village should be handled by the Panchayat Samiti or Zilla Parishad, but with the consent of the Gram Sabha of respective villages.
14. The Gram Sabha/Gram Panchayats must be endowed with administrative and financial resources.
15. The T.D.C. should be given a free hand in procurement and sale of agricultural produce. It should, however, be ensured that T.D.C. works with and for the benefit of the Primary Co-operative Societies in Scheduled Areas for percolating the benefits to Gram Sabha. The T.D.C. should also have a networking to train the tribal people in each village.
16. It is essential to create awareness on the bad effects of consumption of liquor.
17. The procedure of declaration of Gaotham area must be looked into to render useful benefits to the local people.
18. In the Scheduled Areas, a review of Gram Sewaks jurisdiction should be made.
19. The infrastructure under Tribal Sub-Plan should be utilised in a coordinated manner to achieve the objectives of the Extension Act.

ANNEXURES

ANNEXURE-I

SCHEDULED AREAS OF ORISSA (1991 CENSUS)

Sl. No.	District	Details of the tract declared as Scheduled Area	Area of the tract under Scheduled Area (sq.km.)	Total population of the tract covered under Scheduled Areas	Population of Scheduled Tribes in the tract covered under Scheduled Areas	Population of Scheduled Castes in the tract covered under Scheduled Areas
1.	Mayurbhanj	Whole district	10,416.60	18,84,580	10,90,626	1,31,765
2.	Balasore	Nilagiri Block of Nilagiri sub-division	223.60	1,06,468	53,080	10,780
3.	Keonjhar	2 Tehsils of Keonjhar sub-division namely:	5,350.20	6,46,857	3,54,605	52,498
		(i) Keonjhar tehsil				
		(ii) Telkoi tehsil				
		2 tehsils of Champua sub-division namely:	1,585.40	3,28,437	1,52,986	32,487
		(i) Champua sub-division				
		(ii) Barbil tehsil				
4.	Sambalpur	Kuchinda tehsil of Kuchinda sub-division	2,367.30	2,25,086	1,25,741	27,263
5.	Sundargarh	Whole District	9,921.40	1,573,617	798481	138157
6.	Gajapati	(i) R. Udaygiri tehsil of Parlakhemundi sub-division	2,498.80	2,87,799	1,95,495	12,525
		(ii) Guma block of Parlakhemundi tehsil of Parlekhamundi sub-division				
		(iii) Rayagada block of Parlakhemundi tehsil of Parlakhemundi sub-division				
7.	Ganjam	Suruda tehsil excluding Gazalbadi and	912.00	1,42,649	12,852	29,076

(Contd.)

Annexure -I : *(Contd.)*

Sl. No.	District	Details of the tract declared as Scheduled Area	Area of the tract under Scheduled Area (sq.km.)	Total population of the tract covered under Scheduled Areas	Population of Scheduled Tribes in the tract covered under Scheduled Areas	Population of Scheduled Castes in the tract covered under Scheduled Areas
		Gochha Gram Panchayat in Ghumsur sub-division (Bhajanagar)				
8.	Kalahandi	2 blocks namely:	323.80	55,777	31,042	14,170
		(i) Th. Rampur of Bhawanipatna sub-division				
		(ii) Lanjigarh of Bhawani patna sub-division	999.70	60,947	29,832	14,189
9.	Koraput	Whole District	8,534.00	10,29,986	5,21,849	1,38,169
10.	Rayagada	Whole District	7,584.70	7,13,984	4,00,097	1,01,956
11.	Navarangpur	Whole District	5,135.30	8,46,659	4,67,919	1,27,800
12.	Malkangiri	Whole District	6,115.30	4,21,917	2,46,214	84,208
13.	Phulbani	3 Tehsils namely:	2,017.60	1,60,205	76,587	
		(i) Khondmal Tehsil of Khondmal sub-division	2,017.60	1,60,205	76,587	36,180
		(ii) Balliguda Tehsil				
		(iii) G-Udayagiri Tehsil of Balliguda sub-division	5,628.10	3,86,076	2,04,799	63,319
		Total Scheduled Areas	69,613.80	88,71,071	47,62,207 (53.68%)	10,14,542 (11.44%)
		Sub-Total	**1,55,707.00**	**3,16,59,736**	**70,32,214**	**51,29,314**
		Percentage of Scheduled Areas to that of the State	44.70%	28.02%	67.72%	19.78%

ANNEXURE - II

THE PROVISIONS OF THE PANCHAYATS (EXTENSION TO THE SCHEDULED AREAS) ACT, 1996 (NO. 40 OF 1996)

An Act to provide for the extension of the provision of Part IX of the Constitution relating to the Panchayats of the Scheduled Areas.

Be it enacted by the Parliament in the Forty-Seventh year of the Republic of India as follows:

1. This Act may be called the Provisions of the Panchayats (Extension to the Scheduled Areas) Act, 1996.

2. In this Act, unless the context otherwise requires, "Scheduled Areas" means the Scheduled Areas as referred to in clause (I) of Article 244 of the Constitution.

3. The provision of Part IX of the Constitution relating to Panchayats are hereby extended to the Scheduled Areas subject to such exceptions and modifications as are provided in Section 4.

4. Notwithstanding anything contained under Part IX of the Constitution, the legislature of a State shall not make any law under that Part which is inconsistent with any of the following features, namely:

(a) a State legislation on the Panchayats that may be made shall be in consonance with the customary law, social and religious practices and traditional management practices of community resources;

(b) a village shall ordinarily consist of a habitation or a group of habitations or a hamlet or a group of hamlets comprising a community and managing its affairs in accordance with traditions and customs;

(c) every village shall have a Gram Sabha consisting of persons whose names are included in the electoral rolls for the Panchayats at the village level;

(d) every Gram Sabha shall be competent to safeguard and preserve the traditions and customs of the people, their cultural identity, community resources and the customary mode of dispute resolution:

(e) every Gram Sabha shall —

(i) approve the plans, programmes and projects for social and economic development before such plans, programmes and projects are taken up for implementation by the Panchayat at the village level;

(ii) be responsible for the identification or selection of persons as beneficiaries under the poverty alleviation and other programmes;

(f) every Panchayat at the village level shall be required to obtain from the Gram Sabha a certification of utilisation of funds by that Panchayat for the plans, programmes and projects referred to in clause (c);

(g) the reservation of seats in the Scheduled Areas at every Panchayat shall be in proportion to the population of the communities in the Panchayat for whom reservation is sought to be given under Part IX of the Constitution:

Provided that the reservation for the Scheduled Tribes shall not be less than one-half of the total number of seats:

Provided further that all seats of Chairpersons of Panchayats at all levels shall be reserved for the Scheduled Tribes;

(h) the State Government may nominate persons belonging to such Scheduled Tribes as have no representation in the Panchayats at the intermediate level or the Panchayats at the district level:

Provided that such nomination shall not exceed one-tenth of the total members to be elected in that Panchayat;

(i) the Gram Sabha or the Panchayats at the appropriate level shall be consulted before making the acquisition of land in the Scheduled Areas for development projects and before re-settling or rehabilitating persons affected by such projects in the Scheduled Areas; the actual planning and implementation of the projects in the Scheduled Areas shall be coordinated at the State level;

(j) planning and management of minor water bodies in the Scheduled Areas shall be entrusted to the Panchayats at the appropriate level;

(k) the recommendation of the Gram Sabha or the Panchayat at the appropriate level shall be made mandatory prior to grant of prospective licence or mining lease for minor minerals in the Scheduled Areas;

(l) the prior recommendation of the Gram Sabha or the Panchayats at the appropriate level shall be made mandatory for grant of concession for the exploitation of minor minerals by auction;

(m) while endowing Panchayats in the Scheduled Areas with such powers and authority as may be necessary to enable them to function as institutions of self-government, a State Legislature shall ensure that the Panchayats at the appropriate level and the Gram Sabha are endowed specifically with —

   (i) the power to enforce prohibition or to regulate or restrict the sale and consumption of any intoxicant;

   (ii) the ownership of minor forest produce;

   (iii) the power to prevent alienation of land in the Scheduled Areas and take appropriate action to restore any unlawfully alienated land of a Scheduled Tribe;

   (iv) the power to manage village markets by whatever name called;

   (v) the power to exercise control over money-lending to the Scheduled Tribes;

   (vi) the power to exercise control over institutions and functionaries in all social sectors;

   (vii) the power to control over local plans and resources for such plans including Tribal Sub-Plans;

(n) the State legislations that may endow Panchayats with powers and authority as may be necessary to enable them to function as institutions of self-government shall contain safeguards to ensure that Panchayats at the higher level do not assume the powers and authority of any Panchayat at the lower level or the Gram Sabha;

(o) the State Legislature shall endeavour to follow the pattern of the Sixth Schedule to the Constitution while designing the administrative arrangements in the Panchayats at district level in the Scheduled Areas.

5. Notwithstanding anything in Part IX of the Constitution with exception and modifications made by this Act, any provision of any law relating to Panchayats in force in the Scheduled Areas immediately before the date on which this Act receives the assent of the President, which is inconsistent with the provisions of Part IX with such exceptions and modifications shall continue to be in force until amended or repealed by a competent Legislature or other competent authority or until the expiration of one year from the date on which this Act receives the assent of the President:

Provided that all the Panchayats existing immediately before such date shall continue till the expiration of their duration unless sooner dissolved by a resolution passed to that effect by the Legislative Assembly of that State or, in the case of a State having Legislative Council by each House of the Legislature of that State.

ANNEXURE- III

COMPARATIVE ANALYSIS OF EXTENSION ACT AND STATE CONFORMITY ACTS (STATE PANCHAYATS ACT)

Sl. No.	Provisions in Extension Act	Andhra Pradesh	Gujarat	Himachal Pradesh	Madhya Pradesh	Maharashtra	Orissa	Rajasthan
1.	Every Gram Sabha shall be competent to safeguard and preserve the traditions and customs of the people, their cultural identity, community resources and the customary mode of dispute resolution.	Gram Sabha is made competent subject to the condition, "without detriment to any law for the time being in force".	Gram Sabha is competent	Gram Sabha is competent	Gram Sabha is competent	Gram Sabha is made competent subject to the condition, "without detriment to any law for the time being in force".	Gram Sabha is made competent subject to the condition, that customary mode of dispute resolution should be consistent with the "relevant laws in force and in harmony with the tenets of the Constitution and human rights".	Gram Sabha is competent
2.	Every Gram Sabha shall approve the plan programmes and projects before those are taken up for implementation by the Panchayats,	Provisions made	Provisions made	Provisions made	Provisions are made subject to the rules which the	Provisions made	Provisions made	Provisions made

(Contd.)

Annexure III : *(Contd.)*

Sl. No.	Provisions in Extension Act	Andhra Pradesh	Gujarat	Himachal Pradesh	Madhya Pradesh	Maharashtra	Orissa	Rajasthan
	to identify beneficiaries under the poverty alleviation and other programmes and issue certificate of utilisation of funds by the Panchayats for these programmes.				State Government may make in this behalf and subject to the general and special orders as may be issued by the State Government from time to time.			
3.	Prior consultation with Gram Sabha or the Panchayats before making the acquisition or land for development of projects and before re-setting or rehabilitating persons affected by such projects in the Scheduled Area.	With Mandal Panchayats and not with Gram Sabha	With Taluka Panchayats and not with Gram Sabha	With Gram Sabha	Not mentioned except to say that Gram Sabha manages natural resources including land.	With Gram Sabha	With Zilla Parishad	The Gram Sabha or the PRIs at such level as may be prescribed.

(Contd.)

Annexure III : (Contd.)

Sl. No.	Provisions in Extension Act	Andhra Pradesh	Gujarat	Himachal Pradesh	Madhya Pradesh	Maharashtra	Orissa	Rajasthan
4.	Planning and Management of Minor water bodies by Panchayat at appropriate level.	Gram Panchayat, Mandal Panchayat or Zilla Panchayat as the case may be.	Taluka Panchayat	Gram Panchayat, Panchayat	Gram Sabha is to advise Gram Panchayat, Panchayat Samiti or Zilla Parishad as the case may be	Not mentioned	Zilla Panchayat	As may be specified by the State Government or such level as may be prescribed.
5.	Prior recommendation of the Gram Sabha or the Panchayat, at the appropriate level, made mandatory for: (a) Granting of prospecting license or mining lease for minor minerals in the Scheduled Area. (b) Grant of concession for the exploitation of minor mineral by auction.	Gram Panchayat	Gram Panchayat	Gram Sabha	Not mentioned	Every Panchayat (not clear whether it means Gram or Panchayat or Zill Parishad	Zilla Parishad Panchayat Samiti	By the Gram Sabha or the PRIs at such level and in such manner as may be prescribed.
6.	The Panchayat at the appropriate level and the Gram Sabha are endowed specifically with powers to:							

(Contd.)

Annexure III: *(Contd.)*

Sl. No.	Provisions in Extension Act	Andhra Pradesh	Gujarat	Himachal Pradesh	Madhya Pradesh	Maharashtra	Orissa	Rajasthan
(a)	Enforce prohibition or to regulate or restrict the sale and consumption of any intoxicant.	Gram Sabha or the Gram Panchayat as the case may be.	Taluka Panchayat	Gram Sabha or Gram Panchayat as the case may be.	Not mentioned	Gram Sabha	Gram Sabha (to control and supervise and Gram Panchayat to execute).	PRIs at appropriate level or Gram Sabha as may be prescribed.
(b)	Ownership of minor forest produce.	Gram Sabha or the Gram Panchayat as the case may be.	Village Panchayat	Gram Sabha or Gram Panchayat as the case may be.	Gram Sabha or Gram Panchayat as the case may be.	Gram Sabha	Gram Sabha (to control and supervise and Gram Panchayat to execute).	—do—
(c)	Prevent alienation of land in the Scheduled Areas and to take appropriate action to restore any unlawfully alienated land of a ST.	Gram Sabha or the Gram Panchayat as the case may be.	Not mentioned	Gram Sabha or Gram Panchayat as the case may be.	Not mentioned	Gram Sabha (to make recommendations through Panchayat).	—do—	—do—
(d)	Manage village markets	—do—	—do—	—do—	—	—	—	—
(e)	Money-lending to the STs.	Gram Sabha or the Gram Panchayat as the case may be.	Gram Panchayat	Gram Sabha or Gram Panchayat as the case may be.	Gram Sabha (to make recommendations through Panchayat).	Gram Sabha (make recommendations through Panchayat	Gram Sabha (to control and supervise and Gram Panchayat to execute).	PRIs at appropriate level or Gram Sabha as may be prescribed.

(Contd.)

Annexure III : *(Contd.)*

Sl. No.	Provisions in Extension Act	Andhra Pradesh	Gujarat	Himachal Pradesh	Madhya Pradesh	Maharashtra	Orissa	Rajasthan
	(f) Exercise control over institutions and func- tionaries in all social sectors. (g) Control over local plans and resources for such plans including Tribal Sub-Plans.	Mandal Parishad	Taluka Panchayat	Panchayat Samiti	Gram Sabha	Every Panchayat (GP, PS, ZP)	Panchayat Samiti (in consultation with Gram Sabha).	PRIs at appropricate level or Gram Sabha as may be prescribed.
7.	State Legislation shall make necessary provision to enable them to function as insti- tutions of self-government and shall caution safeguards to ensure that Panchayats at the higher level do not assume the power and authority of any Panchayats at the lower level of the Gram Sabha.	No safe- guards are provided in the Act.	No safe- guards are provided in the Act.	No safe- guards are provided in the Act.	No safe- guards are provided in the Act.	No safeguards are provided in the Act.	No safeguards are provided in the Act.	No safeguards are provided in the Act.
8.	The State Lelgislation shall endeavour to follow the pattern of the Sixth Schedule of the Constitution while designing the administrative arrangements in the Panchayats at district level in Scheduled Areas.	No provisions are made.	No provisions are made.	No provisions are made.	No provisions are made.	No provisions are made.	No provisions are made.	No provisions are made.

ANNEXURE–IV

REPORT OF THE COMMITTEE OF MPS AND EXPERTS TO MAKE RECOMMENDATIONS ON THE SALIENT FEATURES OF THE LAW FOR EXTENDING PROVISIONS OF THE CONSTITUTIONS (73RD) AMENDMENT ACT, 1992 TO SCHEDULED AREAS

1. The Ministry of Rural Development, Government of India, constituted a Committee of select Members of Parliament and Experts to make recommendations on the salient features of the law for extending provisions of Part IX of the Constitution to Scheduled Areas. A copy of the order of the Ministry and composition of the Committee are available at Appendix I.

2. The Committee met on 16.7.1994 when it decided to constitute a Group comprising the following members for detailed consideration of the matter and submission of a report to the Committee :

(i) Shri Dileep Singh Bhuria, M.P., Chairman
(ii) Shri Khagapati Pradhani, M.P.
(iii) Prof. M. Kamson, M.P.
(iv) Dr. B.D. Sharma, Expert
(v) Dr. Bhupinder Singh, Expert
(vi) Shri Bandi Oraon, Vice-Chairman, SC/ST Commission
(vii) Smt. Sushma Singh, Joint Secretary (Monitoring), Convenor.

3. The Group met on 25.7.94 and considered the matter from various angles. It decided that a Sub-Group comprising Dr. B.D. Sharma, Dr. Bhupinder Singh and Smt. Sushma Singh should prepare a draft report for the consideration of the Group. The Sub-Group consisting of the three met on 17.8.1994 and discussed the matter in detail from various points of view. They also considered the provisions of different paragraphs of the Sixth Schedule of the Constitution.

4. We are grateful to Dr. Bhupinder Singh, expert member of the Committee, for preparing a number of drafts of the report from time to time. In the final report herewith he has epitomized the discussions and views of the Committee.

The Intent of the Constitutional Amendment Act

5. The Constitution (Seventy-third Amendment) Act, 1992 purports to devolve on Panchayats "such powers and authority as may be necessary to enable them to function as institutions of self-government". Article 243G calls upon the State Govts. to endow powers, authority and responsibilities upon Panchayats with respect to :

(a) preparation of plans for economic development and social justice.
(b) implementation of scheme for economic development and social justice as may be entrusted to them including those in relation to matters listed in the Eleventh Schedule.

5.1 Three tiers of Panchayat *i.e.* at the village, intermediate and district levels have been envisaged though the intermediate level may be dispensed within a State having a population not exceeding 20 lakhs. Election has been prescribed as mode of representation at the village, intermediate and district levels to be conducted by the State Election Commission.

5.2 Reservation of seats has been stipulated for Scheduled Castes and Scheduled Tribes, the number of seats bearing approximately the same proportion to the total number of seats to be filled by direct election in that Panchayat as the population of Scheduled Castes or Scheduled Tribes in that Panchayat area bears to the total population. Similarly, reservation has been made for women, not less than one-third of the total number of seats to be filled by direct election being reserved for women. The offices of chairpersons reserved for Scheduled Castes and Scheduled Tribes should bear the same proportion to the total number of such offices in the Panchayat at each level as the population of Scheduled Castes or Scheduled Tribes bears to the total population of the State. In so far as women are concerned, one-third of the total number of offices of chairpersons in the Panchayats at each level have been reserved for women.

5.3 The normal tenure of a Panchayat has been prescribed as 5 years. Further, a Panchayat has to be reconstituted before the expiry of its tenure or before the expiration of a period of six months from the date of its dissolution.

5.4 The sources of finance of Panchayats have been pin-pointed as :

(i) Such taxes, duties, tolls and fees as are authorized by the State legislature to be collected.
(ii) Such taxes, duties, tolls and fees as are collected by the State Government and assigned to the Panchayats.
(iii) Grants-in-aid to the Panchayats from the consolidated fund of the State.
(iv) Devolution made by the State Finance Commission.

Thus, along with powers and responsibilities, the Act locates specific sources of funding and makes the functioning of Panchayats practical and operational.

5.5 Corresponding provisions exist in "The Constitution Seventy-Fourth Amendment Act, 1993 on Municipalities" applicable to urban areas. It is note worthy, however, that a small number of urban areas fall within tribal areas.

6. An important feature of the Constitution (Seventy-Third Amendment) Act, 1992 through which Part IX comprised of Article 243 to Article 243O, was inserted is that its provisions do not apply automatically to Scheduled Areas and Tribal Areas. Specifically, Article 243M exempts from application of its provision the following :

(i) the functions and powers of the Darjeeling Gorkha Hill Council.
(ii) the States of Nagaland, Meghalaya and Mizoram, each of whose Legislatures may extend the provisions in the State

concerned, barring the tribal areas of Article 244(2).

(iii) the hill areas in the State of Manipur for which district councils exist under any law for the time being in force.

(iv) the Scheduled Areas of Article 244(1) notified as per the Fifth Schedule and tribal areas of Article 244(2) notified as per the Sixth Schedule.

It has to be appreciated that the bulk of tribal population lives in Scheduled Areas and Tribal Areas referred to in category (iv) above. In so far Scheduled Areas and Tribal Areas are concerned, Article 243M (4) (b) makes the provision that Parliament may, by law, extend the provisions of the Act subject to such exceptions and modifications as may be specified in such law and no such law shall be deemed to be an amendment of the Constitution. This shows clearly that the Scheduled Areas, the Tribal Areas and the other three category areas indicated above have been treated on a different footing as compared to rest of the country.

7. At this stage, it is desirable to recapitulate some of the general salient views expressed by the members:

(1) The Constitution presently provides Fifth Schedule for Scheduled Areas all over the country and the Sixth Schedule for some tribal areas of the States of Assam, Meghalaya, Mizoram and Tripura in the north-east region. The major features of the Fifth Schedule are a Tribes Advisory Council, Governor's powers to adapt laws passed by Parliament and State Legislatures and making regulations for the Scheduled Areas having the force of law, and extension of the executive power of the Union Government to the giving of directions to a State for administration, of Scheduled Areas. In contradistinction, the Sixth Schedule deals with constitution of autonomous district councils and autonomous regions specifying for them legislative, judicial, executive, developmental and financial powers and functions. On the whole, the Fifth Schedule provides for Scheduled Area of a State, an enabling frame for legislation in the form of regulations, a tribal consultative machinery in the form of a

Tribes Advisory Council and is paternalistic in its design. It contains the potential to become a potent instrument for prevention of exploitation and discrimination as well as for governance of Scheduled Areas in tribal interest. On the other hand, the Sixth Schedule spells out in different spheres the concept of self-management for autonomous councils and regional councils at the district and regional level respectively. Its focus is on the district level as a unit.

(2) It is note worthy that some tribal areas in the country are covered neither by the Fifth nor the Sixth Schedules of the Constitution. For instance, the hill areas of Manipur State comprising about 90% of the total geographical area of the State is predominantly tribal in demographic character. In Assam also, tribal areas of the State have been left out of both the Fifth and Sixth Schedules of the Constitution. The tribes of north plain of Brahmaputra have been unable to take advantage of constitutional provisions as per the two Schedules. The process of scheduling was commenced in the fifties and was resumed in the seventies as a part of making the Tribal Sub-Plan and Scheduled Areas coterminus. But some-how it has remained incomplete. It is necessary that the remaining Tribal Sub-Plan and MADA areas, as well as similar pockets in West Bengal, Tamil Nadu, Kerala and Karnataka should be covered by Scheduled Areas notification.

(3) The 73rd and 74th Constitution Amendments Acts confer authority on legislatures of States to endow respectively Panchayats and Municipalities with such powers and functions as may be necessary to enable them to act as institutions of self-government. For the purpose, the Panchayats and Municipalities have been charged with the responsibility of preparing and implementing plans for economic development and social justice including those in relation to matters listed in Eleventh Schedule and Twelfth Schedule of the Constitution. In certain respects, the subjects covered by the Eleventh Schedule go beyond functions mentioned for autonomous district councils (ADCs) in the Sixth Schedule. It is, however, pertinent that the bestowal of all or any of the

powers on Panchayats rests with the State Legislatures concerned and is not automatic. In contrast, the powers and functions indicated in the Sixth Schedule are mandatory and do not flow from any further devolution or authorization.

(4) It was emphasized by a number of members that customary law, traditional practices, community ethos etc. should pervade whatever politico-legal-administrative structures are brought into being in Scheduled Areas and Tribal Areas. In fact, the make-up of these structures should be imbued with mode of living, organization, cultural mores etc. of tribal community. A second important facet should aim at combating and preventing exploitation and building up political, economic, social, moral etc. strength of these communities.

(5) The institutions proposed for the Scheduled Areas and Tribal Areas should be vested with adequate competence to deal with emerging problems among tribal people like growing indebtedness, land alienation, deforestation, ecological degradation, displacement on account of industrialization, and modernization, excise policy, alcohol and drug addiction, hydel, water etc. resources. It has to be ensured that access to natural resources in tribal areas remains with the tribal people and they are suitably empowered to utilize them for sustainable development.

(6) Another important aspect concerning institutions under consideration for Scheduled Areas and Tribal Areas is their structure and strength to enable the people in these areas to have access to and command over natural resources. The significance of this aspect will be apparent from the fact that people have been having control over them. While providing access, it is also to be ensured that the proposed institutions are shaped appropriately with a view to utilisation through them of the natural resources for sustainable development.

(7) Note was taken of the fact that in some tribal regions the existing Panchayati Raj System comprising three-tiers of Gram Panchayat, Panchayat Samities and Zilla Parishads have been accepted by the tribal people. But in some other regions the traditional organizational structures and leadership are still

influential. In the latter areas, the Panchayati Raj System has not been a conspicuous success. There is a need, therefore, to ensure that in any system that is proposed traditional systems are allowed to play their due role.

(8) It is also to be recognised that many tribal communities are face-to-face communities and they have been regulating their politico-socio-legal affairs on the basis of principles, procedures, practices, norms, conventions, traditions, precedents etc. as a result of indigenous growth over decades and centuries. As such they find the modern formal systems difficult of understanding and operation. For instance, the choice of leadership among them has been based on informal consensus or selection by the people of the village or the region. Decision-making also has been through consensus rather than by count of votes. These indicate that the traditional practices, processes and procedures of tribal communities have been different from those cast in formal moulds of the present-day systems. It is desirable that the traditional arrangements should not be disturbed. Traditional systems of the Gram Sabha should be accepted. In other words, nothing should be imposed from above on the Gram Sabha which runs counter to the established traditional order, customs, conventions etc.

8. Apart from the views expressed above, some important issues which were raised during the meetings were as follows:

(a) there has to be substantial and meaningful decentralization. The Constitution envisages division of functions between the Centre and the States. But democratic decentralization from the State to the districts and down to the village level, which has been talked of since the past four decades, needs now to be made real. The most significant devolution should occur from the State to the district level and from the district to grass-root tier. The Panchayat Constitutional Amendment Act has laid guidelines for such devolutions for areas other than Scheduled Areas and Tribal Areas. We should evolve appropriate paradigms for Scheduled Areas and Tribal Areas, as per Article 243 (4) (b).

(b) At the grass-root, we should think of an entity which has had, in tribal history, live organic functioning. Rough and hilly topography and thinly populated scattered villages characterise tribal areas. A Gram Sabha represents such an entity at village or hamlet level. Over and above it, a group of villages or hamlets variously called "Parganas" or "Anchal" or "Parha" are found. In the greater part of Central India, the two have been living in homogenous units/conglomerates of socio-political administration. Such administrative arrangements enabled the tribal communities to manage their affairs all through the ages. The traditional organizational set-up based, inter-alia, on physiography, topography etc. should be taken as the basis for a build-up under consideration.

(c) It has also to be recognised that the demographic layout in tribal areas is diverse, varying considerably from region to region. North-Eastern region represents typically its own pattern. On account of topographical features like hills, mountains, streams, rivers, the villages are small and scattered. They could better be described as hamlets. Since these hamlets comprise roughly of 5-30 families each, they have a tendency to aggregate into somewhat bigger units of 5 or 10 hamlets. The bigger unit could be called a village. As such, if a State desires to reckon with 5 or 10 or 15 hamlets as one unit, capped by the district-tier, there should be no objection.

(d) In Central India, at the bottom is Gaon Sabha or Gram Sabha at the hamlet or village level. A group of hamlets/villages may have a Gram Panchayat or Anchal Panchayat or Pargana Panchayat or a Parha Panchayat. Between this second tier and the district-tier, there could be a tier corresponding to a development block. The Panchayat at this intermediate level could be called an Intermediate Council or Janpad Sabha or Taluka Panchayat or Panchayat Samiti. Finally would come the district-tier and the organization at this level could be called the District Council or Zilla Parishad or District Panchayat. But, it has to be emphasized that there is no hard and fast rule about the number of tiers, which has to be decided in the light of conditions prevalent. For instance, the Constitution (Seventy-third Amendment) Act, 1992 prescribes that in a State having a population not exceeding 20 lakhs, the intermediate tier may not be constituted. States in the North-East are characterized by a different set of conditions and they could order their own system.

(e) Notwithstanding the rhetoric of the past four decades, on account of absence of effective democratic decentralization to even district levels, demands and agitations for separate states in the country have taken root in Jharkhand, Bodoland, Uttarkhand etc. Iniquitous policies and actions and economic imbalances have led to resentment among the deprived regions. Assertions on the basis of region, ethnicity, languages etc. have been made. They have come to feel that without the political power of a State, they are not able to claim their rightful due. Further, the feeling has grown that State formation ceased with culturally and economically more powerful segments, while weaker segments have been left out in the cold. Real democratic decentralization may offer to the people some degree of satisfaction. Hence, we should move with urgency in the matter.

(f) A point was made that while there may be force in acceptance and continuance of elements of traditionality blending them with the modern, caution will have to be observed. It will have to be ensured that feudal culture is not encouraged. This point was well-taken: steps need to be taken to allow permeation of the spirit of democracy all over. But, another caution was sounded to the effect that in the name of democracy, the hitherto unified polity of a tribal community should not be allowed to be divided and riven, particularly on party lines. A liberal provision for allowing a tribal community to adopt its own traditions, procedures, norms, ethos etc., would be salutary in this regard.

(g) The essence of the various discussions was that it has to be recognized that in tribal areas society acts like one unit. Unlike in the non-tribal areas, the society is used to prevail over individual view. Hence, in dealing with the tribal societies, this sociological fact has to be kept constantly in view.

9. In Item (e) of the preceding paragraph, we have made a reference to Jharkhand and Bodoland movements. These movements are symbolic of general unrest in tribal areas of the country. It is relevant to recall that the Naxalites movement also had its origin and sweep in the tribal areas during the decades of sixties and early seventies; its adherents are still active in the States of Andhra Pradesh, Orissa, Madhya Pradesh and Bihar. The originators of this movement found fertile ground in tribal areas on account of waves of discontent and unrest in tribal areas. The causes relate to exploitation and discrimination compounded by neglect by those responsible for tribal development and welfare. Comprehensive treatment of the Jharkhand movement may be found in the report of the Committee on Jharkhand Matters (1990) and of the Bodoland movement in the report of the Three-Member Expert Committee (1992).

10. Tribal life and economy, in the not too distant past, bore a harmonious relationship with nature and its endowment. It was an example of sustainable development. But with the influx of outside population, it suffered grievous blows. The colonial system was established on the basis of expropriation of the natural and economic resources of tribal and other areas in the country. Although, theoretically, there has been difference in the approach after the departure of the colonial masters from tribal areas, in practice, the principles enunciated in Article 39 and other Directive Principles of State Policy have to be followed more rigorously. On account of their simplicity and ignorance, over the decades the tribals have been dispossessed of their natural and economic resources like land, forest, water, air etc. The dispossession has not been confined to that through private parties. For the purpose of promotion of general economic development projects, the State also has been depriving them of the basic means of livelihood. These processes have been operative since a long time causing human misery and socio-economic damage. No reliable picture is yet available; for instance,

we are not seized on the total quantum of land alienated from the tribals both on private and State account nor the number of families, clans or tribes involved. This has compelled some to perceive development as an agent of destruction. But since planned development has been an article of faith with us, it has to be ensured that implementation of the policies and programmes drawn up in tribal interest are implemented in tribal interest. Since, by and large, the politico-bureaucratic apparatus has failed in its endeavour, powers should be developed on the people so that they can formulate programmes which suit them and implement them for their own benefits.

11. The report of the Working Group on Tribal Development during the Eighth Plan period is in a way an indictment of the fall-out of the planned development during the last four decades, notwithstanding an unexceptionable objectives and strategy followed in the Tribal Sub-Plan (TSP) concept. The reasons for failure have been spelt out elsewhere a number of times and need not be repeated here. Nevertheless, very broadly, it may be stated that the essentials of the concept have been ignored and mechanical courses followed routinely. In fact, traditional tribal conventions and laws should continue to hold validity. Harmonisation with modern system should be consistent therewith.

Line of Action

12. As already mentioned, Article 243M exempts Scheduled Areas referred to in Article 244(1) and tribal areas referred to in Article 244(2) from application of Part IX *i.e.* the provisions of 73rd Constitution Amendment Act. The Committee was informed that the State Governments have passed legislations for Panchayats as per the provisions of the Constitution (Seventy-third Amendment) Act, 1992. In doing so, they seem to have ignored the exemptions provided for in Article 243M. That is to say the legislations passed by the States apply to the Scheduled Areas of clause (1) of Article 244. We feel that since Article 243M (4) (b) provides for extention of the provisions of Part IX to Scheduled Areas and Tribal Areas by the Parliament subject to such exceptions and modifications as it

may specify in the law passed for the purpose, we feel that Parliament should pass such law. The law passed by Parliament will extend to Scheduled Areas and Tribal Areas to the supersession of the corresponding provisions of State Law. It is the endeavour of this Committee to make suitable recommendations in this report for consideration of the Parliament.

Objects and Reasons

13. Most of the tribal societies in India have been practising democracy, having been characterised by equalitarian spirit. Cognizance has to be taken of their indigenous institutions and ethos while considering democratic decentralisation in tribal areas.

13.1 Time-honoured customary usages and arrangements in tribal areas should be respected and allowed to continue. Traditional tribal conventions and laws should continue to hold validity. Harmonisation with the modern systems should be consistent therewith.

13.2 Panchayati Raj bodies in tribal areas should be made more effective and more participative in the context of the foregoing. More than in the past they have to function as institutions of self-governance and development. They have to work for socio-economic goals for removal of poverty, illiteracy, ill-health etc. among the people.

13.3 For attainment of the aforesaid goals, flow of adequate funds has to be ensured. Such funds should be utilised for the purpose they are set apart and should not be diverted. Suitable financial mechanisms should be created for proper utilization of funds.

13.4 Since the 1992 Act does not take into account the unique features of tribal areas, we make recommendations as embodied in this report.

Role of Fifth and Sixth Schedules

14. There was a general consensus in our meetings that advantage should be taken of both the Fifth and Sixth Schedules in drafting the law under Articles 243M(4) (b). We should interpret the provisions

of the two Amendment Acts as inter-linked with and reinforcing the Fifth and Sixth Schedules, since there is nothing to indicate that they are inconsistent with each other. The Fifth Schedule is to be deemed as a broad and powerful over-arching frame, serving as the fountain-head of essential and beneficial legislation.

Sixth Schedule Frame suitable

15. Flowing from the rationale of the two Constitutional Amendments and drawing sustenance from the Fifth Schedule, a general view has emerged among tribal leaders, representatives and experts that even for the vast Central Indian tribal heartland, with certain changes, the overall design of the Sixth Schedule could serve as a relevant reference frame for a district within the broader canvas of the Fifth Schedule. This view found articulation in our meetings as also in other fora. We understand that in the State of Madhya Pradesh which has already legislated as per directive in the two Acts, a move has been afoot for constituting autonomous district councils in tribal areas as prescribed in the Sixth Schedule of the Constitution. We are aware that in the Central Indian territory, we are dealing with a situation which is qualitatively different from that of the North-East and Sub-Himalayan regions. Though in many districts in Scheduled Areas and north-eastern tribal areas, the tribal population is in majority, non-tribal segments may form a sizeable minority. As such, the functioning of autonomous district councils in the Central Indian areas may be of a different order and kind as compared to what obtains in the North-East. In fact, the district councils may have to be given a deliberate appropriate orientation.

16. This impels us to scan the Sixth Schedule closely, particularly in the light of the fact that sometimes, diametrically opposite views have been expressed in regard to its utility. In the first instance, we refer here to some lacunae we have come across in the Sixth Schedule, those that have marred its working over the years :

(1) The Sixth Schedule focuses itself entirely on the district tier and does not concern itself with tiers under-pinning it. The result is that in some Sixth Schedule areas of the North-East,

no democratic or even sometimes traditional institutionalized tiers are found below it, *i.e.* at the sub-district level.

(2) As per para 16 (2) the power of dissolution of an autonomous district council has not been accompanied by a mandate for reconstitution and hence, is liable to misuse.

(3) There is no express provision that election has to be held within six months of the date of the dissolution of an autonomous district council as provided for in the two Amendment Acts.

(4) According to para 13, the estimated receipts and expenditure pertaining to an autonomous district council are first to be placed before the district council for discussion and thereafter be shown separately in the annual financial statement of the State to be laid before the legislature of State under Article 202. It has been reported that the discussion in an ADC is treated by State authorities as a mere formality leading to the complaint that no real autonomy has been conferred.

These are some outstanding examples of shortcomings in the Sixth Schedule noticed during implementation and they need to be remedied. *But that does not detract from the utility of the Sixth Schedule as a broad charter of autonomy.*

17. In so far as the present matter is concerned, we feel that the aid of the Fifth Schedule should be sought for framing regulations or for any other legislation as may be necessary. The Sixth Schedule is useful for designing an instrument of self-administration at district level for Scheduled Areas.

18. When we consider the Fifth Schedule, we cannot ignore the institutions of Tribes Advisory Council prescribed in para 4 thereof. Such a Council consists of about three-fourths members who are Scheduled Tribe MLAs in the State. The feeling in our meetings was that the record of TACs in the States showed that they have been dysfunctional, by and large. Many of them have not held their meetings regularly. The major problem has been that their contribution to policy-making or monitoring implementation of tribal programmes has not been significant. One view was that with such a record, it is possible that the TAC becomes an obstacle

in the Panchayati Raj structure. However, the other view which prevailed, was that since the TAC is a constitutional body, being a part of the Fifth Schedule, it should not be abolished. On the other hand, action should be taken to reform it and make it functional and workable. For the purpose, it should be able to deal with matters which it thinks are important, in addition to those on which its advice has been sought on reference by the Governor, as indicated in the Fifth Schedule. For instance, currently land alienation, deprivation of tribals of their natural resources, displacement on account of establishment of industrial, mining, hydel etc. projects, are the burning problems of tribals and a TAC should concern itself with these. It should be consulted on legislation to be passed by the State Legislature covering Scheduled Areas and Tribal Areas. When called upon to do so, it may express its view on legislation passed by an autonomous district council within its legislative competence. It should play a more constructive and purposeful part in the overall frame. The Chief Minister should be its Chairman and its meetings should be held quarterly. We suggest that the Fifth Schedule may be amended in the light of these observations to make its role functional.

19. We are aware that there used to be, some time ago, a Central Advisory Council to aid and advise the Government of India in policies, plans, programmes etc. of tribal development and their implementation, monitoring, evaluation etc. This body has been defunct since a long time. The Government of India is deprived of the experience and counsel of a number of important tribal representatives, social scientists, experts, retired administrators, activists etc. We recommend the revival of such a body at the apex of TACs so that the Central Government is enabled to profit from its rich input. In fact, the proposed Central Advisory Council should advise on reference by the Governor in case of difference between the State Government and Tribes Advisory Council or between a District Council and Tribes Advisory Council. In deliberating tribal issues, the Central Advisory Council should keep in view the desideratum of preservation of traditional tribal religious beliefs and practices. Further, its advice should normally be binding. It should be chaired by the Prime Minister and its members may be

Welfare Minister, Home Minister, Rural Development Minister, Deputy Chairman, Planning Commission, etc.

20. We attempt hereunder to delineate broadly our recommendations for a legal frame which could be passed by Parliament. It should be well understood that the law passed by the Parliament will automatically extend to Scheduled Areas and suitable details may be filled in through regulations under the Fifth Schedule.

Salient Features of Proposals

21. Before we enunciate the legal frame, we would like to spell out a few basic premises we regard as important:

(i) The scheme should pre-eminently be related to participative democracy, particularly at the grass-root tiers. Autonomy for institutions under contemplation at the grass-root and district levels should bear a living relationship with the self-management practices which have been in vogue in tribal areas. The autonomy should be non-manipulable.

(ii) The Gaon Sabha or the Gram Sabha at the hamlet/village level should exercise the different functions as traditionally prescribed. More specifically, management of land, forest, water, air etc. resources should be vested in it. This right should be deemed as axiomatic in the functioning of Gram Panchayat, the intermediate Panchayat and the district councils, and also where necessary to be woven into *de jure dicta,* regulations, laws etc. We would like to emphasise harmonious inter-play of forces at the different tiers.

(iii) Many of the present days administrative boundaries were determined during colonial times, based on colonial compulsions. There have been some changes thereafter. But, by and large, the earlier boundaries have stayed with the resulting situation that tribal people are located on borders, be it State, district or block, marginalising them in every way and fragmenting larger communities and areas. State should consider, say within a period of two years, reorganization of the boundaries based on ethnic, demographic and geographic considerations. We feel that these parameters will lead to more rational delimitation.

(iv) In the context of tribal grievances and aspirations, there have been insurgencies, agitations, movements as in North-East, Jharkhand region, Bodoland. We are presently a witness to agitation for Uttarakhand. We feel that tribal aspirations can be satisfied if tribal regions are conferred sub-state status. It may be recalled that Meghalaya had received a sub-state status in 1971. Further, we regard the autonomous district council status for districts in central Indian tribal acts as in the nature of sub-federalism.

(v) The Land Acquisition Act which enables the States to take over any land for "a public purpose", being based on the principle of individual land ownership, does not take cognizance of the customary regulation of common property resources in tribal areas. Among many tribal communities, land and such other natural resources are owned jointly by the community and its use by individuals is sanctioned by the community. In not recognising this basic principle in tribal areas, the Land Acquisition Act is premised on unrealistic ground. The basic lacunae in the Act have to be removed. The consent of the local village community should be obligatory. The rehabilitation package should be operated with the consent of the local village community. Viable and acceptable package of livelihood should be offered as a means of rehabilitation to the affected families. In other words, land should be acquired with the consent of the Gram Sabha, making provision for alternative livelihood for the concerned families acceptable to them.

(vi) It has been observed that the lower functionaries of departments like police, excise, forest, revenue have, generally, been acting against tribal interests and have even become repressive and exploitative. The Committee felt that in the tribal areas, the role of these function*Annexures*aries is minimal, whereas, they tend to over-bear on the tribal and village communities. To eliminate undue interference, the role of police should be minimal and confined to law and order and heinous crimes. The view was expressed that the police should function under the control of ADCs. However, the Home Ministry was of the view that this was not in keeping with the arrangements prevailing in the country. Government servants posted in the autonomous districts should be under the control of the district councils.

(vii) Tribal areas are rich in mineral, forest, hydel, water etc. resources, as a result of which they have been becoming the hub of growth of industries. However, the tribal people have been marginalized in the process of industrialization and urbanization, leading to strong resentment among them. It has been our stand that the tribal community should be regarded as in command of the economic resources. In this view of the matter, in a resource-based industry, the partnership of the village community and the outside capitalist-financiers should be recognized. The district and other councils charged with the responsibility will, no doubt, make appropriate laws for regulation of land and other resources for industries.

Hamlet/Village tier and Gram Sabha

22. The primary unit we contemplate may be a Gram Sabha for a hamlet, or a group of hamlets or a village, as the case may be, in a tribal area. It comprises a face-to-face community managing its affairs in accordance with well-established traditions and customs. The customary codes and procedures should not be disturbed. A hamlet/village comprising a community in a tribal area must be distinguished from a revenue village which is more of an administrative entity. It should be clearly understood that in tribal areas hamlets are more common than big villages. The next level of traditional institutions usually comprises a group of hamlets/villages variously called a Parha or Pargana. In some tribal areas, traditionally village councils have been constituted and at the inter-village level regional councils have been constituted. Both at the village and at the regional level, traditional organizations have been conducting socio-political, economic and judicial affairs. The Gram

Sabha may nominate its executive council, which may be a traditional body. In any event, the wholesome influence, wisdom and experience of the older generation should not be discounted, particularly since the reins of affairs have been, for aeons, in their hands.

Gram Panchayat

23. For a group of hamlets/villages i.e. for an Anchal or Parha or Pargana, it should be a Gram/Anchal/Parha Panchayat, composed of elected representatives.

24. The foregoing formulation would lead to a participative hamlet/village tier and a formal Gram Panchayat tier. This is necessitated by the topographical and demographic conditions in the tribal areas, as already explained. It should, however, be understood that there cannot be any hard and fast rule prescribing the number of tiers in all the districts. The physiographic, topographic, demographic etc. conditions vary from State to State.

Intermediate Panchayat

25. The next i.e. intermediate tier Panchayat in tribal areas may be the same as elsewhere in the country, variously called Panchayat Samiti, Janpada Sabha, Taluka Panchayat etc. co-terminus with a development block area.

Autonomous District Council

26. The next level i.e. the district requires close examination. Presently, as a part of the three-tier structure, Zilla Parishads exist in many States of the country. We have also the examples of several North-Eastern States which, with entrenched democratic structures and practices, have been able to do well with traditional village and district-level formations, as in Nagaland, Mizoram. But in so far as the generality of tribal areas in the other parts of the country is concerned, it would appear that the dominant bureaucratic apparatus at the district-level has hardly touched any tribal chord. It is in this

context that we mark to the structure of autonomous district councils contained in the Sixth Schedule of the Constitution in force in the States of Assam, Meghalaya, Mizoram and Tripura. The Sixth Schedule was conceived by the farmers of the Constitution to be an instrument of socio-economic development and self-management of hill tribal communities inhabiting the districts. The self-management was expected to satisfy ethnic aspirations of the tribal communities. It cannot be gain-said that it has fulfilled that goal to a larger or smaller extent. While we wish that the self-management concept be adopted for the Central Indian Tribal areas, we feel that the seats in the district council may be filled up by election, carving out constituencies appropriately in the district. However, some scope could be retained for nomination in the district council of representatives of certain minority tribal communities who cannot come through the election process, through setting apart seats not exceeding five in number for representation of such minority communities, to be filled up in consultation with the Governor.

27. We know of certain districts which are not tribal-majority districts, in the sense that Scheduled Tribe people do not constitute more than 50 per cent of the total population of the district. But the STs are concentrated in a part or parts of the district, say in some blocks or a sub-division or sub-divisions. If the tribal population in these units is substantial in absolute terms, there is no reason why analogus arrangements should not be ushered in such areas. Councils to be formed for such areas could be termed as Autonomous Sub-District Councils (ASDCs). ASDCs should be conferred powers and functions at par with those of ADCs. However, this may be regarded as an interim arrangement, pending reorganization of administrative boundaries which we have recommended elsewhere in this report. As we have mentioned there, the reorganization should be completed within a couple of years.

28. We have envisaged a Village council/Gram Sabha, Anchal council, Intermediate council and District council. But there could be in addition to these area councils. For instance, in the State of Bihar there had been Chotanagpur and Santhal Parganas Authority now trifurcated into three authorities. Under contemplation in the Jharkhand region, is an area council.

29. The Group considered the question of association of MLAs and MPs with the intermediate (block) Panchayats and district councils. The 1992 Constitution Amendment Act provides for representation of the members of the House of the People and members of the Legislative Assembly of the State representing constituencies which comprise wholly or partly a Panchayat area, at a level other than the village level. The consensus which emerged was that it is desirable to associate Scheduled Tribe MLAs and MPs for many reasons in the district and intermediate Panchayats. Though the two function at State and national levels respectively, they remain in touch with the grass-roots level. Their presence in the councils of the two upper tiers would, as a result, be doubly advantageous i.e. for the grass-roots views to be reflected at the State and national levels and for the national and State level policies to be transmitted to the district and sub-district levels. It was, however, felt that, from the national level, the representation should be limited to Scheduled Tribe Lok Sabha members. From the State level, this restriction my not be applied and MLAs whose constituencies fall within the jurisdiction of the intermediate and district councils may find place in the two tiers.

30. The Group was further of the view that notwithstanding the fact that the areas under consideration i.e. Scheduled Areas are expected to have majority of tribal population, it is necessary to stipulate that the Panchayats therein will have a majority of Scheduled Tribe members. The reasons is that the Scheduled Areas were notified as such on account of majority of Scheduled Tribe population, contiguity etc. In course of time, on account of influx of non-ST population, in a few Scheduled Areas, the status of the ST population might have been reduced to minority. That should not be regarded to have altered the over-all character of the Scheduled Areas. The chairman and vice-chairman should belong to Scheduled Tribes. One-third of the seats should be reserved for women.

31. In para 5 supra, we made reference to some features of the Constitutional Amendment. At this juncture, we wish to reiterate that an elected Panchayat should be reconstituted within six months of the dissolution of an existing one. Further, that the act of dissolution should not be taken lightly; should be based on substantial, serious

and convincing evidence like malfeasance or anti-national, anti-constitutional etc. nature. Moreover, it should be ordered by the Governor. We presume that the question of dissolution is and will remain justiciable.

Assignment of subjects to Panchayats

32. To the Constitution Seventy-third (Amendment) Act, 1992 on the Panchayats has been appended the Eleventh Schedule which contains subjects assigned by the two Acts respectively to the Panchayats and the Municipalities. Further, Article 243G of the former Act and 243W of the latter confer on the Legislature of the State authority to endow Panchayats with such powers and authority as may be necessary to enable them to function as institutions of self-government and for preparation and implementation of plans for economic development and social justice. It is seen that the items contained in the Scheduled are of wide-ranging nature.

33. The Sixth Schedule of the Constitution which is a charter for autonomy for some tribal areas of the North-East, assigns a number of functions for the district councils of those tribal areas. We have given careful thought to the question as to the most suitable pattern for the councils at the district level. As we have mentioned earlier, the Sixth Schedule confers powers of legislation and administration of justice on the district councils apart from the executive, developmental and financial responsibilities. We note that the Panchayats and Municipalities of the 73rd and 74th Amendment Acts, have been entrusted with such wide-ranging responsibilities. We are of the view that we should adopt for districts in Scheduled Areas and Tribal Areas the Sixth Schedule format but expand it to include subjects that are indicated in the two Acts. Further, that the village community, that is at the level of Gram Sabha, should have the responsibility of safeguarding the rights of tribals in matters relating to land, water, forest, minor forest produce etc. They should be vested with the power to regulate and use community land, forest (other than reserve forest), water, air and other natural resources, local schools, dispensaries, roads, ferries, markets etc. Government servants serving in the respective

Panchayats should be under their control. The right to mineral leases should be pre-empted in favour of the community.

34. A communitarian and cooperative spirit among the tribals and tribal communities has been a conspicuous feature. When modern societies have been shedding such a spirit in favour of individualism, many tribal societies have been able to retain it. It is manifested in a number of their undertakings like shifting cultivation, house construction. Not usually accustomed to joint working, members of the formal administration have been oblivious of the advantages of cooperative endeavours. There is need to pay attention to this attribute ingrained among tribal individuals and collectivities. We suggest that the Panchayats which will come into being as a result of the law of Parliament to be enacted in accordance with Article 243M (4) (b), should pay adequate attention to this aspect. We are aware that cooperatives have been created in tribal areas by the administration, including LAMPS. But we are of the view that these cooperatives did not have much chance of a success due to their formal structure, rigid procedures and certain underlying assumptions. The tribal societies have been run on oral traditions and general presumption of trust in each other. We hope that the Panchayats will be enabled to establish cooperative organizations suitable to the tribal milieu, capturing the innate tribal sensibilities.

Legislative

35. The legislative powers of an Autonomous District Panchayat should extend to the following:

(a) the allotment, occupation or use or the setting apart, of land, other than any land which is a reserved forest for the purposes of agriculture or grazing or for residential or for any other non-agricultural purposes or for any other purpose likely to promote the interests for the inhabitants of any village or town:

Provided that nothing in such laws shall prevent the compulsory acquisition of any land, whether occupied or unoccupied, for purposes of defence, railways, roads, educational and health institutions by the Government of the State concerned in accordance with the law for the time being in force authorizing such acquisition.

(b) Management of forest

(c) Management of minor forest producc

(d) Management of water resources

(e) Regulation of practice of shifting cultivation

(f) Establishment of town committees or councils and their powers

(g) Matters relating to village or town administration including village or town Police

(h) Appointment or succession of chiefs or heads

(i) Customary law including inheritance, marriage, divorce etc.

(j) Local customs

(k) Control of money-lending, and trading by non-tribals

(l) Excise

(m) Laws regarding partnership of local communities in enterprises based on local resources.

As provided for in the Sixth Schedule, laws made relevant to the above subjects will have to be approved by the Governor of the State.

36. The Committee was emphatic that such laws should be enforced as would prevent further alienation of the tribal land. The principle of evidence should be that the onus of proof of the member of a non-ST community having acquired the land legitimately should lie on that member and not on the ST transferor. There should also be an embargo on sale of tribal land by authorities, since often times STs are trapped into situations due to their ignorance of law and realities, the Scheduled Areas and Tribal Areas, land should be transferable only to members of Scheduled Tribes, irrespective of whether the transferor is a member of Scheduled Tribe or not.

Administration of Justice

37. It has been observed that modern legal system creates wedge between people and parties, while traditional systems bind the people in societal and fraternal ties. In fact, the legal and conventional jury-based systems evolved by the tribal (or sometimes other rural) communities have kept these communities going for ages. Their virtues should be squarely conceded and the traditional legal bodies should be recognized to enable to continue to function. There should be no police interference in cases under adjudication by traditional bodies. In other words, in so far as administration of justice is concerned, in all matters other than those for which the Governor may confer powers on a court, it should continue to be dispensed with, as at present, by the traditional bodies which exist mostly at the village and inter-village levels. The police should take cognizance or entertain complaints in respect of matters within the jurisdiction of the Gram Sabha only when the Gram Sabha so directs for reasons adopted in a resolution. Law officers should be trained in tribal customary law and, if found fit, they should be posted to assist tribal juries.

Executive

38. In para 6 of Sixth Schedule, executive, regulatory and development functions have been indicated for the District Council. It is pertinent to compare them with 29 items mentioned in the Eleventh Schedule (Annex-III). It will be advantageous to include all the items mentioned in para 6 (1) of the Sixth Schedule and the Eleventh Schedule.

39. Paras 8 and 9 of the Sixth Schedule are regulatory in character, the former dealing with the power to assess and collect land revenue and to impose taxes and the latter dealing with share of royalties accruing from licenses or leases for the purpose of prospecting for or extraction of minerals. This provision should be kept for thè ADCs.

40. In tribal areas the occurrence of urban conglomerates is not as common as in non-tribal areas. Nevertheless, wherever they occur, it is found that tribal pockets within such a conglomerate

are more or less administratively autonomous. This needs to be given due recognition. Further, municipalities and notified area councils and other such bodies should function under the overall control of district autonomous councils. However, this will need examination in the light of the Seventy-fourth Constitution Amendment Act.

Financial

41. The Panchayat and Municipalities Acts provide for the following sources of finances:

(a) Through levy of collection of taxes, duties, tolls and fees [Article 243H(a)]
(b) Assignment by the State Government of such taxes, duties tolls and fees as are levied and collected by the State Governments.
(c) Grants-in-aid to the Panchayats from the Consolidated Fund of the State.
(d) Devolution of financial awards by a State Finance Commission (Article 243I).

42. Compared thereto, the provision in the Sixth Schedule is simpler. The only source of finance it contemplates is from the Consolidated Fund of the State. As indicated earlier, this provision has not been adequate and not working satisfactorily.

43. It needs to be recalled that the Constitution has, in the first proviso to Article 275(1), a specific provision for promotion of welfare of Scheduled Tribes or raising the level of administration of Schedule Areas with the help of funds to be paid out of the Consolidated Fund of India as grants-in-aid to the State. This provision has been sparingly used. Now that Panchayats in tribal areas are being conceived *de novo*, there is no reason why this provision should not be used for allocating to them finances for schemes of tribal development and administration of Scheduled Areas, both for plan and non-plan purposes. It should be understood clearly, however that recourse to this provision should not debar Scheduled Areas and Tribal Areas from receiving other funds like

Articles under 243H and 243I. Further, management and utilization of financial resources assigned to the panchayats should be within the competence of these bodies. Funds may be received by the district councils directly from the Central and State Governments and distributed among the lower-tier panchayats.

44. We have indicated above the source of funds and financial mechanisms. We recommend that for the purposes of tribal development, welfare, administration etc., the funds from whatever source derived and linked to whatever mechanisms, should be placed in "charged" category as opposed to "voted" category. We understand that placement of funds in "charged" category enables certain advantages. For instance, it does not permit of diversion or use elsewhere, nor of reduction in quantum. Once the funds are placed in "charged" category in the budget, they remain intact and are available for only the purpose for which they were included in the budget. We make this suggestion as we have heard of a large number of examples which indicate that funds for tribal development even in the Tribal Sub-Plan were diverted or misused. We hope that by keeping the earmarked funds in "charged" class of budget, they will be used in a sacrosanct manner.

45. Further, in order to prevent wrong financial practices occurring in the Tribal Sub-Plan field, Tribal Sub-Plan funds (whether relating to State plan or special Central assistance or any other) pertaining to different sectors of development should be quantified and placed at the disposal of the autonomous district councils for distribution among the Panchayats in the districts. Moreover to the extent possible, the Central and State Governments should devise procedures for direct allotment of funds to the district autonomous councils.

46. Education and health have been regarded as very important sectors for Scheduled Tribes. In fact, some tribal leaders and experts hold the view that education should be accorded primacy in prioritization of different sectors in the development spectrum. Nevertheless, in actual practice, the two sectors have not been given their due. We feel that, in keeping with the felt needs, education and health sectors should be the first charge on the part of the Panchayats.

Appointment of Commission

47. Para 14 of the Sixth Schedule is to the effect that the Governor may, at any time appoint a commission to examine and report on any matter relating to the administration of autonomous district councils. The retention of such a provision for Scheduled Areas of the country will be useful. However, the chairman and members should be chosen carefully and representation should be given to Scheduled Tribes.

48. It should be provided that the autonomous district councils (Panchayats) being contemplated should review the existing laws for their relevance and applicability and take such action as is necessary for exclusion of those that are irrelevant and inclusion of those that are useful. The Governor of the State may issue a notification for the purpose to ensure that such review and action is completed within a stipulated period, say two years.

49. We find that the States have already passed legislations in pursuance of the 73rd Constitution Amendment Act. We understand that the provisions of those legislations apply to Scheduled Areas and Tribal Areas also. We have in this report made recommendations for Scheduled Areas for consideration by the Parliament. The law as passed by the Parliament will be applicable to Scheduled Areas. Regulations could be framed under the Fifth Schedule by the Governor as and when necessary. Further, representatives may be chosen/elected to the Panchayat bodies on the basis contained in Parliament's law to be enacted. The existing administrative boundaries of blocks and districts should be readjusted to conform to the requirements of geographic, ethnic and tribal areas.

50. For Scheduled Areas, we propose that a Gram Sabha may be conferred powers and functions as in Annexure 'A' herewith, the Gram Panchayat the powers and functions included in Annexure 'B', a Panchayat Samiti or Janpad Sabha the powers and functions referred to in Annexure 'C' and an Autonomous District Council as in Annexure 'D'. The powers and functions relate to the fields of legislation, administration of justice, general administration, finance etc. We, however, envisage these as a first step.

51. We understand that some reservations have been expressed by certain Ministries in regard to certain provisions which we have suggested in this report, which may appear unconventional. They may be due to inadequate appreciation of the tribal situation and the constitutional scheme for creating a system which accords well with the tribal milieu. It may also be recalled that the Constitution envisages a structure for tribal areas (which includes Scheduled Areas) "notwithstanding anything in the Constitution".

52. We have dealt in this report with proposals and provisions that we think should apply to the Fifth Schedule Areas in the country as declared by the President under para 6 of that Schedule. Article 243M introduced by the Constitution Seventy-third Amendment Act, 1992 covers also "tribal areas referred to in clause (2) of Article 244". These areas have been specified in the Sixth Schedule of the Constitution as follows:

PART– I

(1) The North Cachar Hills District
(2) The Karbi Anglong District

PART – II

(1) Khasi Hills District
(2) Jaintia Hills District
(3) The Garo Hills District

PART – II (A)

Tripura Tribal Areas District

PART – III

(1) The Chakma District
(2) The Mara District
(3) The Lai District

We feel that the benefit of self-government at different tiers should be made available to these areas. In this report, we are not making any rccommendations in detail in regard to the sub-district Panchayat organizations for these areas. We feel that this matter is better left to be considered separately. But, since we have examined the Sixth Schedule for the purpose of its applicability to the Fifth Schedule Areas and since we have already highlighted its advantages and shortcomings, we suggest that the framework of the Sixth Schedule be examined afresh in the light of our suggestions in the Annexure'D'. The amended framework in Annexure'D' may be helpful for reformulation.

Summary of Recommendations

1. The Committee has been called upon to suggest:

(a) Steps for harmonization of Fifth, Sixth, Eleventh and Twelfth Schedules of the Constitution as they impinge upon the Panchayati Raj Institutions;
(b) Salient features of the law that may be taken up for enactment by Parliament for extending the provisions of the part IX of the Constitution to the Scheduled Areas referred to in clause (1) of Article 244 of the Constitution subject to such exemptions and modifications as may be necessary under Article 243 M(4) (b); and
(c) Variations and modifications in other articles relevant to the Fifth Schedule Areas in order to strengthen institutions of local Government in Fifth Schedule Areas.

2. The Committee felt that while certain provisions of "The Constitution Seventy-third Amendment Act, 1992 on the Panchayats" were wholesome and should be incorporated in the law to be passed by Parliament under Article 243M (4) (b), certain unique characteristics of tribal societies and tribal areas need to be kept in view. Important among them are that many tribal societies have had their own customary laws, traditional practices, community ethos, political and administrative systems etc. In considering the

aforesaid law, their mode of living, organization, cultural mores, etc. and their present-day predicament of exploitation, deprivation, marginalisation etc. would have to be kept in focus. Since many tribal communities have been living autonomously cut off from the rest of the society, they have exercised control over and had access to natural resources moulding their institutions. Their Gram Sabhas and village councils have been vibrant institutions in the administrative, religious, political, economic, justice etc. fields. The Committee felt that while shaping the new Panchayati Raj structure in tribal areas, it is desirable to blend the traditional with the modern by treating the traditional institutions as the foundation on which the modern supra-structure should be built.

3. As per article 243(4)(b) Parliament may, by law, extend the provisions of Para IX to Scheduled Areas and tribal areas covered by clause (1) and clause (2) respectively of Article 244 subject to such exemptions and modifications as may be specified in such law. Parliament may consider our recommendations for such legislation. The law passed by Parliament will be applicable to Scheduled Areas and Tribal Areas to the supersession of corresponding provisions of any State laws.

Objects and reasons

4. Most of the tribal societies in India have been practising democracy, having been characterized by egalitarian spirit. Cognizance has to be taken of their indigenous institutions and ethos while considering democratic decentralization in tribal areas.

4.1 Time-honoured customary usages and arrangements in tribal areas should be respected and allowed to continue. Traditional tribal conventions and laws should continue to hold validity. Harmonisation with the modern systems should be consistent therewith.

4.2 Panchayati Raj bodies in tribal areas should be made more effective and more participative in the context of the foregoing. More than in the past they have to function as institutions of self-governance and development. They have to work for socio-economic goals for removal of poverty, illiteracy, ill-health etc. among the people.

4.3 For attainment of the aforesaid goals, flow of adequate funds has to be ensured. Such funds should be utilized for the purpose they are set apart and should not be diverted. Suitable financial mechanisms should be created for proper utilization of funds.

4.4 Since the 1992 Act does not take into account the unique features of tribal areas we make recommendations as embodied in this report.

5. In drafting the law under Article 243 (M) (4) (b), advantage should be taken of both the Fifth and Sixth Schedules. The Fifth Schedule should be deemed as a broad and powerful overarching frame, serving as the fountain-head of essential and beneficial legislation. The design and contents of the Sixth Schedule could serve as a relevant reference frame for a district within the broader canvas of the Fifth Schedule. However, ethnic, regional and other related variations should be given due consideration. The Sixth Schedule should be regarded with such reformation and changes as are necessary, as a broad charter of autonomy at the district level and be adopted.

6. The Tribes Advisory Council, envisaged by the Fifth Schedule as a consultative body at the State level, needs to be reformed to make it an effective and functional organization. The Chief Minister of the State should be its Chairman and its meetings should be held once every three months.

7. At the Centre, the Central Advisory Council should be revived, serving the purpose of (a) a sounding board for tribal policies and programmes, and (b) advice in disputes between a State Government and the Tribes Advisory Council or between a District Council and the Tribes Advisory Council. Its advice should normally be binding. The Prime Minister should chair its meetings and its members may be Welfare Minister, Home Minister, Rural Development Minister, Deputy Chairman, Planning Commission, etc.

8. Many of the present-day administrative boundaries were determined during colonial times. Notwithstanding changes, by and large, the earlier boundaries have stayed. Reorganisation of boundaries based on geographic, ethnic and demographic

considerations may be considered and finalized within a couple of years.

9. The tribal societies are characterised by a communitarian and a cooperative spirit, visible in many undertakings like shifting cultivation, house construction. The potential of this ingrained attribute has not been taken advantage of so far. Cooperative organizations among tribals should be constituted suitable to their oral traditions and milieu.

10. It has been observed that in tribal areas the lower functionaries of departments like Police, Excise, Forest, Revenue have generally been acting against tribal interests and not unoften have even become repressive and exploitative. While their role in tribal areas is minimal, they tend to over-bear on the tribal and village communities. Hence, they should be assigned minimal role and should work under the control of concerned Panchayats.

11. The 1992 Act envisages a Panchayat at village level in addition to Panchayats at intermediate and district levels, as per Article 243B. The concept of Panchayat at village level may fit in well for non-tribal areas, since villages there are generally large. But in tribal areas, with mostly hilly topography, the villages are usually scattered and population-wise small. These small villages or hamlets, are known as "Tolas" in some areas. But a small village or group of hamlets or habitations may have its own Gram Sabha. The Gram Sabhas should be allowed to exercise their customary traditional role unhindered. Further, a Gram Sabha may have a traditional village council which performs varied functions – religious, political, economic, judicial etc. – on its behalf. The Gram Sabha may nominate its executive council or village council, which may be a traditional body and may delegate to it functions like execution of development works.

12. A number of hamlets aggregated may constitute a village Panchayat, called variously a Gram Panchayat or Anchal or Parha or Pargana Panchayat. This tier corresponds to the lowest tier envisaged in the 1992 Act. Its members may be elected.

13. Constituencies may be delimited for election of members to the intermediate and district tier Panchayats. The district level Panchayat may be called Autonomous District Council (ADC)

14. In certain districts, scheduled tribe population may be less than 50% of a district's total population, but it may be concentrated in a part or parts of the district, say in some blocks or a sub-division or sub-divisions. We have recommended that sub-district councils may be constituted for such areas and designated as Autonomous Sub-District Councils (ASDCs). ASDCs should be at par with ADCs. However, this may be regarded as an interim arrangement, pending reorganization of administrative boundaries which we have recommended elsewhere.

15. So far as the organizational structure of an ADC is concerned, we recommend adoption of the broad frame-design of autonomous district councils contained in the Sixth Schedule of the Constitution in force in the States of Assam, Meghalaya, Mizoram and Tripura. The Sixth Schedule has been conceived to be an instrument of self-management and socio-economic development. It may not be too far wrong to say that, to an extent, it has fulfilled the ethnic aspirations of tribal communities. We have enumerated in this Report (Para 16) some shortcomings of the Sixth Schedule and these would need to be reformed. In addition, we feel that some scope should be opened up through setting apart seats (may be not exceeding 5 in number) for nomination in the district council of minority tribal communities, who cannot find place through the election process. The nominations may be in consultation with the Governor.

16. The 1992 Constitution Amendment Act provides for representation of Members of the House of People and Members of the Legislative Assembly of the State, representing constituencies which comprise wholly or partly a Panchayat area, at a level other than the villages level. We recommend that Lok Sabha Scheduled Tribe MPs should be associated at the intermediate (Block) Panchayat and the District Council. But the representation should not be restricted to Scheduled Tribe MLAs and even non-ST MLAs should be associated in the two tiers.

17. Since the Scheduled Areas and Tribal Areas and expected to have majority of tribal population, the different tier Panchayats therein should have majority of Scheduled Tribe Members. Further, both the chairman and vice-chairman should belong to STs.

18. The Sixth Schedule confers powers of legislation and administration of justice on the district councils apart from the executive, developmental and financial responsibilities. We should adopt for districts in Scheduled Areas the Sixth Schedule format, but expand it to include subjects that are indicated in the Eleventh Schedule of the Constitution.

19. The legislative powers of the autonomous district councils in the Fifth Schedule Areas have been proposed more or less on the same lines as in the Sixth Schedule, with some amendments. In so far as administration of justice is concerned, the Committee has been emphatic that a traditional jury-based legal system evolved by tribal societies should be recognized and should be enabled to continue to function. There should be no police interference in cases not involving non-heinous offences. Such cases should be under the domain of the Gram Sabha. In so far as development functions are concerned, this also is a vital area, our proposal is that the functions enumerated in the Sixth Schedule as well as in the Eleventh Schedule should be discharged by the ADCs. We have given a list of such functions in Annexure 'D'.

20. In Article 243H, the sources of funds for Panchayats have been detailed. These should be applicable to Panchayats in Scheduled Areas. While the Panchayats in these areas may receive funds as per Articles 243H and 243I, funds as per the first proviso to Article 275(1), should continue to be available normally.

21. For the purposes mentioned in the first proviso to Article 275(1), funds received from other than the Panchayats own, should be placed in "charged" category in the respective governments' budgets as opposed to "voted" category. This will enable funds to remain fully available for purposes related to tribal interest, without fear of mis-utilisation or diversion.

22. In order to prevent wrong financial practices occurring in the Tribal Sub-Plan field, the Tribal Sub-Plan funds (whether relating to State plan or special Central assistance or any other) pertaining to different sectors of development should be quantified and placed at the disposal of the Autonomous District Councils for distribution among the Panchayats in the district. Moreover, to the extent possible, the Central and State Governments should devise

procedures for direct allotment of funds to the Autonomous District Councils.

23. Education and health sectors should be the first charge on the funds received by a Panchayat in Scheduled Areas and, notwithstanding any other provision, the Panchayat will have power to appropriate funds from any other head for meeting this obligation.

24. All government servants and functionaries of institutions concerned with the functions of a Panchayat in a Scheduled Area and located within its jurisdiction will be under its control.

25. As per the provision in the Sixth Schedule, the Governor may appoint a Commission to examine and report on all matters relating to the administration of autonomous district councils. Representation should be given to Scheduled Tribes in the membership of the Commission.

26. The Tribes Advisory Councils and Autonomous District Councils in the Scheduled Areas should review the existing laws for their relevance and applicability and take action necessary for exclusion of those that are relevant and inclusion of those that are useful. Such action should be completed within a stipulated period of about two years.

27. We understand that States have already passed legislation in pursuance of the Seventy-third and Seventy-fourth Constitution Amendment Acts and that the provisions of those laws apply to Scheduled Areas also. The law passed by the Parliament will supersede such and any other related law.

28. The process of scheduling of tribal areas in the country commenced earlier has remained incomplete. It is necessary that the remaining Tribal Sub-Plan and MADA areas as well as similar other pockets should be included in the Scheduled Areas.

29. We have dealt in this report with proposals and provisions that we think should apply to the Fifth Schedule Areas in the country as declared by the President under para (6) of that Schedule. Article 243M of the 1992 Act covers "tribal areas referred to in clause (2) of Article 244". We feel that the benefit of self-government at different tiers should be made available to these areas. We leave this matter to the judgement of the States concerned. But, since we have examined the Sixth Schedule, we suggest that the

framework of that Schedule should be looked afresh in the north-eastern region in the light of our suggestions contained in Annexure 'D'. The reformed framework in Annexure 'D' may be helpful for reformulation.

30. We recommend for the Gram Sabhas, Gram Panchayats, Intermediate Panchayats and Autonomous District Councils powers, functions and procedures enumerated respectively in Annexures 'A', 'B', 'C' and 'D'.

APPENDIX-I

No.N-11011/3/93-PR
Government of India
Ministry of Rural Development
Krishi Bhawan, New Delhi
the 10th June, 1994

ORDER

Subject : Constitution of a High Level Committee to make recommendations on the salient features of the law for extending the provision of the Constitution (73rd Amendment) Act, 1992 to the Scheduled Areas.

It has been decided to constitute a High Level Committee to discuss and examine the issues relating to extension of the provisions of Part IX of the Constitution to the Scheduled Areas and to make recommendations on the salient features of the laws for extending the provisions of this Part of the Constitution to the Scheduled Areas.

2. Accordingly, a High Level Committee is hereby constituted with the following composition:

1.	Shri Dileep Singh Bhuria, M.P.	Chairman
2.	Shri Shibu Soren, M.P.	Member
3.	Shri Bheru Lal Meena, M.P.	Member
4.	Shri Khagapati Pradhani, M.P.	Member
5.	Shri Somjibhai Damor, M.P.	Member
6.	Shri Manikrao H. Gavit, M.P.	Member
7.	Shri Piyus Tirkey, M.P.	Member
8.	Prof. M. Kamson, M.P.	Member
9.	Mrs. K. Kamla Kumari, M.P.	Member
10.	Shri Mankuram Sodhi, M.P.	Member
11.	Shri S.N. Brohmo Chaudhury, M.P.	Member
12.	Shri Peter G. Marbaniang, M.P.	Member

13.	Mrs. Bibhu Kumari Devi, M.P.	Member
14.	Shri Hiphei, M.P.	Member
15.	Shri Sushil Barongpa, M.P.	Member
16.	Shri Bandi Oraon, Vice-Chairman, SC/ST Commission	Member
17.	Dr. B.D. Sharma, Formerly Commissioner for SC/ST, Govt. of India	Member
18.	Dr. Bhupinder Singh, Formerly Spl. Commissioner for SC/ST, Govt. of India	Member
19.	Shri D.N. Tiwari, Director General, Forest Research Institute, Dehradun	Member
20.	Dr. R.L. Meena, Addl. Secretary, Deptt. of Legal Affairs	Member
21.	Shri P.K. Mohanty, Joint Secretary, Ministry of Welfare	Member
22.	Smt. Sushma Singh, Joint Secretary, Ministry of Rural Development	Member Convenor

3. The terms of reference of this Committee would be as under :

(a) The Committee shall suggest steps for harmonization of Fifth, Sixth, Eleventh and Twelfth Schedules of the Constitution as they impinge upon the Panchayati Raj Institutions.

(b) It shall formulate the salient features of the law that may be taken up for enactment by Parliament for extending the provisions of the Part IX of the Constitution to the Scheduled Areas referred to in clause (I) of Article 244 of the Constitution subject to such exemptions and modifications as may be necessary under Article 243 M(4) (b); and

(c) Variations and modifications in other Acts relevant to the Fifth Schedule Areas in order to strengthen institutions of local Government in Fifth Schedule Areas.

4. The Committee would submit its recommendations within a period of three months.

5. The Committee will lay down its own procedure and methodology of work.

6. The secretarial assistance and related services to the Committee would be provided by the Ministry of Rural Development.

(Sushma Singh)
Joint Secretary to the Government of India

To

1. All members of the Committee.
2. The Cabinet Secretariat, Rashtrapati Bhavan, New Delhi.
3. Shri K.R. Venugopal, Secretary, Prime Minister's Office, South Block, New Delhi.
4. The Secretary, Ministry of Parliamentary Affairs, 42, Parliament House, New Delhi.
5. PS to MOS (RD) (T)/PPS to Secy (RD)/PS to AS (RD).
6. Guard file/spare copies.

ANNEXURE 'A'

POWERS, FUNCTIONS AND PROCEDURES PROPOSED FOR GRAM SABHA IN TRIBAL AREAS

A. (1) Safeguard of the rights of tribal individuals, tribal communities and Gram Sabhas in matters relating to land, water, forest and minor forest produce;

(2) Enforcement of customary rights and Nishtar over natural resources such as grazing, fuel, fodder, minor forest produce, building materials;

(3) Powers to manage, regulate and use community land, water, air and forest (other than reserve forest);

(4) People's mobilization for community welfare prorgrammes and organizing voluntary labour for community works;

(5) Arranging contributions in cash and kind for public purposes;

(6) Promotion of solidarity and harmony among all sections of people irrespective of religion, faith, caste, creed or race;

(7) Guide and advise the Gram Panchayats in regard to schemes for economic development and social justice;

(8) Consideration of the budget and action plan of the Gram Panchayat and preparation of report thereon;

(9) Consideration of report on the audit of accounts of the Gram Panchayat;

(10) Preparation of the Gram Sabha budget, annual and five-year plan programmes;

(11) Laying down principles for identification and identification of schemes required to be taken up on priority basis for economic development;

(12) Laying down principles for identification and identification of beneficiaries for poverty alleviation and other programmes;

(13) Constitution of one or more beneficiary committees comprising not more than 9 persons for ensuring active

participation of people in implementation, maintenance and equitable distribution of benefits of schemes in the area;

(14) Arranging for cultivation of land lying unused and bringing wastelands under cultivation;

(15) Women and child development;

(16) Consideration of requisitions for land acquisition for purposes other than defence, railways, roads, education and health institutions and approval of schemes of rehabilitation acceptable to the affected persons. Implementation of the scheme of rehabilitation;

(17) Drinking water supply;

(18) Sanitation, conservancy and drainage;

(19) Public health measures;

(20) Village roads and streets;

(21) Small tanks;

(22) Maintenance of public properties and community assets;

(23) Preservation and approval of all matters covering traditional practices, customs, usages and arrangements;

(24) Execution of small works of development like drinking wells, irrigation, wells, housing, village roads through agency or agencies as it deems appropriate;

(25) Regulation of manufacture, sale and consumption of intoxicants.

(26) Management of local institutions like schools, dispensaries, health sub-centres, Aganwadis, cooperative stores and outlets, Hats.

(27) Cognizance and adjudication of all civil disputes including debts and other liabilities and criminal offences not being heinous crimes like murder, dacoity;

(28) Appointment of the village council and delegation to it of powers;

(29) Regulation of money-lending and trading.

B. (1) Not less than 50% of the total number of members shall form a quorum for a meeting of Gram Sabha. No quorum shall be necessary for an adjourned meeting which will be held at the same time and place after seven days;

(2) A meeting of the Gram Sabha shall be presided over by the headman of the village or in his absence a member of the Sabha chosen by them;

(3) All questions coming before a Gram Sabha shall be discussed and points raised therein shall be referred to the Gram Panchayat for its consideration;

(4) The proceedings of the meetings of the Gram Sabha shall be recorded by such person or persons as may be authorized by the Presiding Officer;

(5) The Gram Sabha shall conduct its business through such traditional agencies or councils as customary. It may also set up executive committees like a village council for the transaction of business, execution of works etc;

(6) The Gram Sabha shall hold its meetings as frequently as necessary, the frequency being not less than one meeting per month on a fixed date. At such meetings, it may record its objections to any action of Sarpanch/Pradhan or any other member of Gram Panchayat for failure to implement any development scheme properly or without active participation of the people.

C. (1) All funds for discharge by the Gram Sabha of the aforesaid functions shall be provided to it by the concerned authorities;

(2) The Gram Sabha shall ensure proper utilization and disbursement of funds to the concerned beneficiaries;

(3) Education and health sectors shall be the first charge on the funds received by the Gram Sabha and, notwithstanding any other provision, the Gram Sabha will have power to appropriate funds from any other head for meeting this obligation;

(4) Certification of utilization of funds shall be the responsibility of the Gram Sabha.

D. (1) All government servants and functionaries of other institutions concerned with the functions of the Gram Sabha and located within its jurisdiction will be under its control.

ANNEXURE 'B'

POWERS, FUNCTIONS AND PROCEDURES OF GRAM PANCHAYATS

A 1. A Gram Panchayat shall function as a unit of self-government and, in order to achieve economic development and secure social justice for all, shall, subject to such conditions as may be prescribed or such directions as may be given by the ADC :

(a) prepare a development plan for the five-year term and revise and update it as and when necessary with regard to the resources available;

(b) prepare an annual plan for each year by the month of October of the preceding year for development of human resources, infrastructure and civic amenities in the area;

(c) implement schemes for economic development and social justice as may be drawn up by, or entrusted to it; and

(d) implement the enactments or decisions of ADC

2. (a) The Gram Panchayat shall prepare in the prescribed manner a report of the work done during the previous year and the work proposed to be done during the following year and submit it to the prescribed authority and to the Panchayat Samitis concerned within the prescribed time;

(b) The Gram Panchayat shall, in October and April every year, prepare a half-yearly report showing the amount received by the Gram Panchayat during the previous half-year from different sources including the opening balance and the amount actually spent on different items of work and a list of beneficiaries. The report and the list shall be published immediately for preparation in the office of the Gram Panchayat for information of general public;

(c) The Gram Panchayat shall, as soon as may be after the

preparation of the report and the list, place the same in the meeting of Gram Sabhas for discussion and adoption with modifications, if any, and shall furnish copies of the report as modified to the prescribed authorities and the Panchayat Samiti by middle of January every year; and

(d) The Gram Panchayat shall guide and support the Gram Sabhas in such manner as may be necessary.

3. Without in any way affecting the functions of the Gram Sabha, the Gram Panchayat shall have powers to undertake schemes and shall adopt measures in respect of :

(a) Use of community lands, water, forest (other than reserve forest), air;
(b) Rural development programmes;
(c) Primary, social, adult or non-formal education;
(d) Rural dispensaries, health centre, maternity and child welfare centres;
(e) Agriculture including agricultural extension and fuel and fodder;
(f) Irrigation including minor irrigation, water management and watershed development;
(g) Improved breeding of cattle, medical treatment of cattle and prevention of cattle disease;
(h) Rural housing programme;
(i) Rural electrification including distribution of electricity;
(j) Non-conventional energy sources;
(k) Management of public ferry;
(l) Management of Hats, markets;
(m) Rehabilitation of displaced persons;
(n) Women and child development;
(o) Acting as a channel through which Government's assistance reaches villages;
(p) Implementation of such scheme as may be formulated or performance of such acts as may be entrusted to the Gram Panchayat by the State Government; and

(q) Field publicity on matters connected with development works and other welfare measures taken by the State Government.

4. The duties and responsibilities of a Gram Panchayat shall be -

(a) to provide within the area under its jurisdiction supply of drinking water, cleansing and disinfecting source of supply and storage of water;
(b) Sanitation, conservancy and drainage and prevention of public nuisance;
(c) Curative and preventive measures in respect of malaria, filaria, small-pox, plague or any other epidemic;
(d) Maintenance, repair and construction of streets and protection thereof;
(e) Protection and repair of buildings or other properties vested in it;
(f) Management and care of public tanks, public toilets, crematoria and graveyards;
(g) Organising voluntary labour in community works;
(h) Imposition, assessment and collection of taxes, rates or fees to be levied;
(i) Construction and regulation of markets;
(j) Protection and encouragement of cottage industries and food processing industries;
(k) Promotion of dairy and poultry;
(l) Poverty alleviation programmes;
(m) Maintenance of public distribution system;
(n) Maintenance of community assets; and
(o) Fostering of endogenous institutions.

B.1 (a) Every Gram Panchayat shall hold a meeting at least once a month in the office of Gram Panchayat. Such a meeting shall be held on such day and such hour as the Gram Panchayat may fix at the immediately preceding meetings. All meeting of the Gram Panchayats shall be open meetings;
(b) The Sarpanch or the Pradhan or, in his absence, the Naib Sarpanch or Up-pradhan shall preside at the meeting of

the Gram Panchayat. In the absence of both, the members present shall elect one of them to be the president of the meetings;

(c) One-third of the total number of members, subject to a minimum of three members shall form a quorum for a meeting. Provided that no quorum shall be necessary for an adjourned meeting; and

(d) All questions coming before a Gram Panchayat shall be decided by a majority of votes. Provided that in case of equality of votes, the persons presiding shall have a second or casting vote.

C. (1) The Gram Panchayat shall hear appeals in respect of cases arising out of decisions of the Gram Sabha and, for the purpose, it will constitute a standing body of Panchas, including traditional leaders, held in esteem for their integrity. Their decision will be final.

(2) The Gram Panchayat shall also hear and decide inter-village disputes.

D. (1) All government servants and functionaries of other institutions concerned with the functions of the Gram Panchayat and located within its jurisdiction will be under its control.

(2) Education and health sectors shall be the first charge on the funds of the Gram Panchayat and, notwithstanding any other provision, the Gram Panchayat will have power to appropriate funds from any other head for meeting this obligation.

ANNEXURE 'C'

POWERS, FUNCTIONS AND PROCEDURES OF INTERMEDIATE PANCHAYATS

A. 1. An Intermediate Panchayat shall function as a unit of self-government and, in order to achieve economic development and secure social justice for all shall, subject to such conditions as may be prescribed or directions as may be given by the ADC.

(a) Prepare a five-year development plan and revise and update it as and when necessary with reference to the resources available;
(b) Prepare an annual plan for each year by the month of January of the preceding year for development of human resources, socio-economic advancement of the community, provision or reinforcement of the infrastructure, attention to civic amenities in the area etc;
(c) Arrange to have the plans, programmes and schemes included in the five year and annual plans implemented through the concerned agencies;
(d) Comply with the decisions and enactments of ADC; and
(e) Examine and sanction the budget estimates of Gram Panchayats in its jurisdiction.

2. The intermediate Panchayat shall prepare in the prescribed manner a report on the work done during the previous year and the work proposed to be done during the following year and submit it to the prescribed authority, the Gram Panchayats within its jurisdiction and the ADC concerned, within the prescribed time;

3. A Panchayat Samiti shall have the following powers and functions

(a) Foster tribal endogenous institutions;

(b) Coordinate and integrate the development plans and schemes prepared by the Gram Panchayats in the block, with particular reference to the resource-potential of the area, the skills, aptitude and occupations of the people and availability of funds;

(c) Ensure compliance with the principle and contents of Tribal Sub-Plan;

(d) Supervise and ensure proper functioning of Hats and tribal cooperatives (LAMPS or by any other name called);

(e) Manage forest and forest resources including minor forest produce;

(f) Undertake schemes or adopt measures, including the giving of financial assistance relating to development of agriculture, fisheries, live-stock, Khadi, cottage and small-scale industries, co-operative movement, rural credit, water supply, irrigation and minor irrigation including water management and watershed development, public health and sanitation including establishment and maintenance of dispensaries and hospitals, communication, primary and secondary education, adult and non-formal education, welfare of students, social forestry and farm forestry including fuel and fodder, rural electrification including distribution, non-conventional energy sources, women and child development, social welfare and other objects of general public utility;

(g) Manage or maintain any work of public utility or any institution vested in it or under its control and management;

(h) Make grants-in-aid of any school, public institution or public welfare organization within the Block;

(i) Adopt measures for relief of distress;

(j) Undertake execution of any scheme, performance of any act, or management of any institution or organization entrusted to it by the State Government or any other authority;

(k) Contribute such sum or sums as it may decide, towards the cost of water-supply or anti-epidemic measures undertaken by a municipality within the Block;

(l) Make grants to the District Council or Gram Panchayats.

4. A scheme shall normally be executed by the Gram Panchayat which has jurisdiction, unless the Panchayat Samiti and/ or Gram Panchayat are of the opinion that implementation of such a scheme is beyond its competence, financially or otherwise and a resolution or resolutions are passed to that effect. In the latter case, the Intermediate Panchayat may execute the scheme itself or entrust its execution to the Gram Panchayat and give such assistance as may be required.

5. An Intermediate Panchayat may undertake or execute a scheme if it extends to more than one Gram Panchayat.

6. An Intermediate Panchayat shall exercise general power of supervision and control over Gram Panchayats in the block and it shall be the duty of the concerned authorities to give effect to the directions of the Panchayat Samiti.

B 1. An Intermediate Panchayat shall hold a meeting in its office at least once every three months on such date and such hour as the Panchayat may fix at the immediately preceding meeting.

2. One-fourth of the total number of members shall form a quorum for a meeting. Provided that no quorum shall be necessary for an adjourned meeting.

3. All questions coming up before Intermediate Panchayat shall be decided by a majority of votes. Provided that in case of equality of votes, the person presiding shall have second or casting vote.

4. An Intermediate Panchayat may set up Working Committees to look after different aspects like planning, finance, agriculture, cooperation, land reforms, education, small industry and electrification.

5. (a) An Intermediate Panchayat shall, at such time and in such manner as may be prescribed prepare in each year a Budget of its estimated receipts and disbursement for the following year and submit to the ADC having jurisdiction;

(b) The District Council may, within such time as may be prescribed, either approve the budget or return it to the Intermediate Panchayat for such modification as it may direct. On such modifications being made, the budget shall be re-submitted within such time as may be prescribed for approval of the Council. If the approval of the Council is not received by the Panchayat Samiti by the last date of the year, the Budget shall be deemed to have been approved by the Council.

C. (1) The Panchayat Samiti shall hear appeals in respect of inter-village disputes and its decision will be final.

D. (1) All government servants and functionaries of other institutions concerned with the functions of the Panchayat Samiti and located within its jurisdiction will be under its control.

(2) Education and health sectors shall be first charge on the funds of the Panchayat Samiti and, notwithstanding any other provision, the Panchayat Samiti will have the power to appropriate funds from any other head for meeting this obligation.

ANNEXURE 'D'

POWERS, FUNCTIONS AND PROCEDURE PROPOSED FOR AUTONOMOUS DISTRICT COUNCIL

Consistent with the powers and functions conferred on Gram Sabha, Gram Panchayat and Intermediate Panchayat respectively in Annexures 'A', 'B' and 'C', the District Autonomous Councils will have powers and functions enumerated hereunder.

A. Legislative

1. (a) Allotment, occupation or use or setting apart of land other than land which is reserved for forest for the purpose of agriculture or grazing or for residential or other non-agricultural purposes or for any other purpose likely to promote the interests of inhabitants of any village or town. Provided that nothing in such laws shall prevent the acquisition of any land, whether occupied or unoccupied, for the purposes of defence, railways, roads, educational and health institutions run by the Government of the State concerned in accordance with the law for the time being in force authorizing such acquisition;
   (b) The management of any forest not being a reserved forest;
   (c) The use of any canal or water-course for the purpose of agriculture;
   (d) The regulation of the practice of Jhum or other forms of shifting cultivation;
   (e) The establishment of town committees or councils and their powers;
   (f) Any other matter relating to town administration including town police and public health and sanitation;
   (g) The appointment or succession of chiefs or headmen;
   (h) Inheritance of property;

(i) Marriage and divorce;
(j) Social customs;
(k) Cooperatives.

2. Regulation and control of money-lending or trading within the district by persons residing in the area. Such a regulation may;

(a) Prescribe that no one except the holder of a license issued in his behalf shall carry on the business of money-lending;
(b) Prescribe the maximum rate of interest which may be charged or be recovered by the money-lender;
(c) Provide for the maintenance of accounts by money-lenders and for the inspection of such accounts by officers authorized by the ADC;
(d) Prescribe that no non-resident of the district shall carry on any trade, whether wholesale or retail, except under a valid license issued by the ADC.

3. Excise policy like enforcing prohibition or regulating or restricting the sale and consumption of any intoxicant.

4. All laws made under this paragraph shall be submitted forthwith to the Governor and, until assented to by him, shall have no effect.

5. No act of Legislature of the State in which an ADC is located in respect of any of the matters specified in item 1 above as matters with respect to which an ADC may make laws shall apply to the autonomous districts unless the District Council for that district by public notification so directs, and the District Council in giving such direction with respect to any act may direct that the act shall, in its application to that district have effect subject to such exceptions or modifications as it thinks fit.

6. (a) If, at any time, the Governor is satisfied that an Act or resolution of a District Council is likely to endanger the safety of India or it is likely to be prejudicial to public order, he may annul or suspend such Act or resolution and take such steps as he may consider necessary (including

suspension of the Council and the assumption of all or any of the powers vested in or exercisable by the Council) to prevent the commission or continuance of such Act or coming into effect of such resolution;

(b) Any order made by the Governor in clause (a) above together with the reasons thereof shall be laid before the Legislature of the State as soon as possible and the order shall, unless revoked by him, continue in force for a period of twelve months from the date on which it was made.

Provided that if any so often as a resolution approving the continuance in force of such order is passed by the Legislature of the State, the order shall, unless cancelled by the Governor, continue in force for a further period of twelve months from the date on which it would have otherwise ceased to operate.

7. All laws, rules and regulations made by a District Council shall be published forthwith in the official Gazette of the State and shall on such publications have the force of law.

B. Administration of Justice

1. An Autonomous District Council (ADC) may constitute, to the exclusion of any court in the State, court or courts comprising a jury and a law officer, for trial of suits and cases other than those which are within the jurisdiction of the Gram Sabha and those which the Governor may specify. The Council may appoint suitable persons as presiding officers of such courts. They may also appoint officers necessary for administration of laws made in accordance with the legislative powers of ADC.

2. The District Council may appoint a court of appeal in respect of suits and cases triable by courts referred to in the preceding paragraph.

3. The High Court shall exercise such jurisdiction over the suits and cases mentioned in the foregoing as the Governor may, from time to time, by order specify.

4. The District Council may, with the previous approval of the Governor, make rules regulating :

(a) constitution of courts and appellate courts and the powers to be exercised by them;
(b) the procedure to be followed by such courts in trial of suits and cases;
(c) enforcement of decisions and orders of such courts;
(d) any ancillary matter.

5. The Governor may, for the trial of suits or cases arising out of any law in force in an autonomous district or for trial of offences punishable with death, transportation for life or imprisonment for a term of not less than seven years under the Indian Penal Code or any other law applicable, confer on a court constituted by the district council, such powers under the Code of Civil Procedure, 1908 of the Code of Criminal Procedure, 1898 as he deems appropriate.

C. Executive

1. The District Council may in general, exercise all functions in the executive field which flow from legislative powers enumerated in section 'A' above.

2. Matters relating to rights of tribals over land, water, forest (including minor forest produce), air etc. shall be within its jurisdiction.

3. An Autonomous District Council (ADC) shall function as a unit of self-government and, in order to achieve economic development and secure social justice for all, shall prepare:

(a) a development plan for the five-year term, and
(b) an annual plan for each year by the month of January of the preceding year in furtherance of its objectives of development of the community as a whole and socio-economic upliftment of the individual members of the community.

4. The ADC shall have the power to advise the State Government on all matters relating to the development work among Gram Panchayats and Intermediate Panchayats.

5. It shall have power to :

(i) undertake schemes or adopt measures including the giving of financial assistance relating to the development of agriculture, fisheries, livestock, Khadi, cottage and small scale industries, cooperative movement, rural development, water supply, irrigation and minor irrigation including water management and watershed development, public health and sanitation including establishment and maintenance of hospitals, communication, primary and secondary education, adult and non-formal education, physical education and games and sports, welfare of students, social forestry and farm forestry including fuel and fodder, rural electrification including distribution, non-conventional energy sources, women and child development, social welfare and other objects of general public utility;

(ii) undertake execution of any scheme, performance of any act, or management of any institution or organization entrusted to it by the State Government or any other authority;

(iii) manage or maintain any work of public utility or any institution vested in it or under its control and management;

(iv) make grants to the intermediate Panchayats and Gram Panchayats;

(v) coordinate and integrate the development plans and schemes prepared by Intermediate Panchayats in the districts;

(vi) examine and sanction the budget estimates of Intermediate Panchayats in the district; and

(vii) adopt measure for the relief of distress.

6. An ADC shall not undertake or execute any scheme confined to a block unless the implementation of such scheme is beyond the competence of the Intermediate Panchayat concerned financially or otherwise. But an ADC may undertake or execute any scheme if it extends to more than one block.

7. It may constitute sufficient number of Standing Committees for consideration of proposals and implementation of schemes under specific programmes.

D. Financial

1. The District Council shall have the authority to frame its budget in respect of all receipts and expenditure. In doing so, it shall observe all budgetary procedures.

2. All funds receivable by an ADC from the Central or State Governments shall be placed in the "charged" category in the respective budgets of the Central and State Governments.

3. The estimated receipts and expenditure pertaining to an autonomous district which are to be credited to, or to be made from, the Consolidated Fund of the State shall be first placed before the District Council for discussion and then after such discussion be shown separately in the annual financial statement of the State to be laid before the Legislature of the State under Article 202.

4. Consolidated District Fund

(a) There shall be constituted for each autonomous district, a Consolidated District Fund to which shall be credited all moneys received respectively by the District Council for that district in the course of administration of such district in accordance with the provisions of this Constitution;

(b) Education and health sectors shall be the first charge on the Consolidated Fund and, notwithstanding any other provision, the ADC will have power to appropriate funds from any other head for meeting this obligation.

(c) The Governor may make rules for the management of the Consolidated District Fund and for the procedure to be followed in respect of payment of money into the said Fund, the withdrawal of moneys therefrom, the custody of moneys therein and any other matter connected with or ancillary to the matters aforesaid;

(d) The accounts of the District Council shall be kept in such form as the Comptroller and Auditor-General of India may, with the approval of the President, prescribe; and

(e) The Comptroller and Auditor-General shall cause the accounts of the district to be audited in such manner as he may think fit, and the reports of the Comptroller and Auditor-General relating to such accounts shall be submitted to the Governor who shall cause them to be laid before the Council.

5. Powers to assess and collect land revenue and to impose taxes

(a) The District Council for an autonomous district in respect of all lands within the district shall have the power to assess and collect revenue in respect of such lands in accordance with the principles for the time being followed;

(b) The District Council for an autonomous district in respect of all areas in the district shall have power to levy and collect taxes on lands and buildings, and tolls on persons resident within such areas;

(c) The District Council for an autonomous district shall have the power to levy and collect all or any of the following taxes within such district, that is to say –
- — taxes on professions, trades, callings and employments.
- — taxes on animals, vehicles and boats.
- — taxes on the entry of goods into a market for sale therein, and tolls on passengers and goods carried in ferries.
- — taxes for the maintenance of schools, dispensaries or roads.

(d) District Çouncil may make regulations to provide for the levy and collection of any of the taxes and every such regulation shall be submitted forthwith to the Governor and, until assented to by him, shall have no effect.

6. Licences or leases for the purpose of prospecting for, or extraction of, minerals

(a) Such share of the royalties accruing each year from licences or leases for the purpose of prospecting for, or the extraction of, minerals granted in respect of any area within an autonomous district as may be agreed upon between the Government of the State and the District Council of such district shall be made over to that District Council.

(b) If any dispute arises as to the share of such royalties to be made over to a District Council, it shall be referred to the Governor for determination and the amount determined by the Governor in his discretion shall be deemed to be the amount payable under sub-paragraph (a) of this paragraph to the District Council and the decision of the Governor shall be final.

E. General

1. The Governor may on the recommendation of a Commission appointed in his behalf by public notification order the dissolution of a District Council and

(a) direct that a fresh election shall be held immediately for the reconstitution of the Council, or

(b) subject to the previous approval of the Legislature of the State assume the administration of the area under the authority of such Council himself or place the administration of such area under the Commission appointed or any other body considered suitable by him for a period not exceeding six months.

Provided that when an order under clause (a) of this paragraph has been made, the Governor may take the action referred to in clause (b) of this paragraph with regard to the administration of the area in question pending the reconstitution of the Council on fresh general election.

Provided further that no action shall be taken under clause (b) of this paragraph without giving the District Council an opportunity of placing as views before the Legislature of the State.

2. If, at any time, the Governor is satisfied that a situation has

arisen in which the administration of an autonomous district cannot be carried on in accordance with the provisions of the Constitution, he may, by public notification, assume to himself all or any of the functions or powers vested in or exercisable by the District Council and declare that such functions or powers shall be exercisable by such person or authority as he may specify in his behalf, for a period not exceeding six months.

Provided that the Governor may by a further order or orders extend the operation of the initial order by a period not exceeding six months on each occasion.

3. Every order made under sub-paragraph (2) of this paragraph with the reasons therefor shall be laid before the Legislature of the State and shall cease to operate at the expiration of thirty days from the date on which the State Legislature first sits after the issue of the order, unless, before the expiry of that period, it has been approved by the State Legislature.

4. Election to constitute an ADC shall be completed before the expiry of its normal duration of five years or before the expiration of a period of six months from the date of its dissolution. Provided that where the remainder of the period for which a dissolved Panchayat would have continued is less than six months, it shall not be necessary to hold any election under this clause for constituting it for such a period.

5. The Governor may at any time appoint a Commission to examine and report on any matter specified by him relating to the administration of autonomous districts. Such a Commission should have due representation of Scheduled Tribe members on it.

QUESTIONNAIRES

Questionnaire - I

Research Project on Panchayati Raj in Scheduled Areas: A Critical Study

States: Andhra Pradesh, Bihar, Gujarat, Himachal Pradesh, Maharashtra, Madhya Pradesh, Orissa and Rajasthan

	Current and Future Obstacles	Remedial Measures
1. Power Sharing.		
2. Commitment to decentralisation of power.		
3. Traditional Tribal Councils.		
4. Exploitative practices and employment.		
5. Access to basic resources.		
6. Violence against STs and unrest in tribal areas.		
7. Tribal Sub-Plan (See Article 244, Fifth Schedule and list of Schedule Areas) Co-terminus with Tribal Sub-Plan area but MADA/ Clusters excluded.		
8. Poverty.		
9. Access to education, health, drinking water, etc.		
10. Key cultural impediments.		

11. Administrative framework.

12. Training needs (different categories) availability, trainers, backlog.

13. PRIs and women and children. (See State Policy for women)

Questionnaire - II

Research Project on Panchayati Raj in Scheduled Areas: A Critical Study

States: Andhra Pradesh, Bihar, Gujarat, Himachal Pradesh, Maharashtra, Madhya Pradesh, Orissa and Rajasthan

The provisions of the Panchayats (Extension to the Scheduled Areas) Act, 1996
(No. 40 of 1996, 24 December 1996)
An Act to provide for the extension of the provisions of Part IX of the Constitution relating to Panchayats of the Scheduled Areas

1. Has the Act been enforced, if so since when? Obtain copy of the Order?
2. Has the State Government made any rules to give effect to provisions of the Act?
3. There are other State and Central Acts having bearing on the Panchayats (Land allotment, alienation, money-lending, forest conservation, etc.) How are these reconciled for coordinated results?
4. Role of Tribal Advisory Council.
5. Is the legal frame adequate?
6. NGO role.
7. Delegation of Power.
8. Programme Transfer.
9. The Act enjoins Gram Sabha to be endowed specifically with certain powers like:

(a) the power to enforce prohibition or to regulate or restrict the sale and consumption of any intoxicant;

(b) the ownership of minor forest produce;

(c) the power to prevent alienation of land in the Scheduled Areas and to take appropriate action to restore any unlawfully alienated land of a Scheduled Tribe;

(d) the power to manage village markets by whatever name called;

(e) the power to exercise control over money-lending to the Scheduled Tribes;

(f) the power to exercise control over institutions and functionaries in all social sectors;

(g) the power to control local plans and resources for such plans including Tribal Sub-Plans.

What is the local status?

10. Any comments/observations.

Questionnaire - III

Research Project on

Panchayati Raj in Scheduled Areas: A Critical Study

States: Andhra Pradesh, Bihar, Gujarat, Himachal Pradesh, Maharashtra, Madhya Pradesh, Orissa and Rajasthan

Guided Schedule/Questionnaire for use at Gram Sabha/ Panchayat Level

1. Please obtain from Panchayat Office a profile of the Gram Sabha incorporating (a) area; (b) population — SC/ST/OBC/ men/women, etc.; (c) when the last elections held; (d) when are the next elections due; (e) results in a tabular form; (f) name of SC/ST women members, Sarpanch/Mukhya, etc.; (g) Problems and prospects of the area.
2. Ask people (Tribals) : Are they in groups aware :
   (1) About the Panchayat in general.
   (2) Main benefits of the 1996 Act.
3. Are development programmes done through Gram Sabha/ Panchayats?
4. Access to people for placing their views.
5. An assessment of the working of the Panchayats.
6. What according to them are the three important items of priority needs in the Gram Sabha/Panchayat:
   (a) Employment.
   (Nature of it can be spelt out)
   (b) Drinking Water.

(c) Link roads.

(d) Marketing of agricultural produce, MFP, etc.

(e) Education.

(f) Health.

(g) Stopping exploitation.

7. Is there any difficulty with quorum in Panchayat meetings?
8. Are women members co-operative in the funcioning of Panchayats?
9. Does guidance come by?
10. Any complaint?

Questionnaire - IV

Research Project on

Panchayati Raj in Scheduled Areas: A Critical Study

States: Andhra Pradesh, Bihar, Gujarat, Himachal Pradesh, Maharashtra, Madhya Pradesh, Orissa and Rajasthan

Schedule in its original or any modified form to be canvassed at various level of State Government Administration as secondary information base

A. State HQ/District HQ/SDO/BLK

1. Concept of separate provisions for Scheduled Areas [Article 243 (M)] — views and comments of senior officers/experts/ministers/MLAs/MPs.
2. Bhuria Committee's Report — Any observation.
3. Preparedness of Scheduled Tribes to implement the provisions.
4. Preparedness of the Administration to implement the Act 1996.
5. Working of Tribal Sub-Plan.
6. Administration of Scheduled Areas, especially anti-exploitative measures like land transfer, money-lending, liquor vending, MFP trade.
7. Co-operation of people, their perception.
8. Role of NGOs.
9. Priorities in tribal development *vis-a-vis* Panchayat role.
10. Vast areas of tribal concern like restoration of basic resources (land, water, forests) environmental degradation, unemployment, non-implementation of labour and forest Acts, etc. Role of the Panchayat.

11. Copies of Acts, orders, rules.
12. Reports of any research assessment, evaluation study within last three years.
13. Maps.
14. Photographs.
15. Pamphlets.

Important :

Arrange for as many group discussions as possible of different sections of people and discuss and keep note of views on issues listed above and locally relevant.

Questionnaire - V

Research Project on

Panchayati Raj in Scheduled Areas: A Critical Study
States: Andhra Pradesh, Bihar, Gujarat, Himachal Pradesh, Maharashtra, Madhya Pradesh, Orissa and Rajasthan

The Study sponsored by the Ministry of Social Justice and Empowerment (Tribal Development Division) has the following main features :

1. Whether the Panchayats in the Scheduled Areas in the States of Andhra Pradesh, Bihar, Gujarat, Himachal Pradesh, Madhya Pradesh, Maharashtra, Orissa and Rajasthan have been endowed with such powers and authority as may be necessary to enable them to function as institutions of self-government, as envisaged in the 1996 Act.
2. If so, the details.
3. If not, the reasons and comments thereof.
4. The nature, functions and role of Gram Sabhas to discharge functions specified in the 1996 Act.
5. To suggest measures to achieve the goals, envisaged in extending the provisions of Part IX of the Constitution.
6. Study all other related issues *vis-a-vis* Tribal Sub-Plan mechanism, administrative structure, etc., in relation to Panchayati Raj in Scheduled Areas and make recommendations.

Questionnaire - VI

Research Project on

Panchayati Raj in Scheduled Areas: A Critical Study
States: Andhra Pradesh, Bihar, Gujarat, Himachal Pradesh, Maharashtra, Madhya Pradesh, Orissa and Rajasthan

Basic data/information to be collected from the field (Gram Sabha, Panchayat)

Description of Gram Sabha (Village, Taluk, Panchayats, Blocks)

1. When constituted?
2. (a) Population – SC/ST/OBC

   (b) Voters – Male........ Female...........
3. Meetings held during two years – 1, 2, 3

   Date of the meetings: In 1998 :

   In 1999 :
4. Important decisions taken at the above meetings :
5. Details of items of work done during 1997, 1998, 1999
6. Major basic needs of the area in order of priority :

   1.

   2.

   3.
7. Any conflict or misunderstanding with neighbouring Gram Sabha/Panchayat on any item like sharing of irrigation water, forest produce, electricity, etc.
8. Most important infrastructure needed – Road, Bridge, Canal.

9. The three-tier systems :
    (a) Gram Sabha/Village
    (b) Block
    (c) Zila working OK?
10. How cordial is the relationship between government (executive officers, etc.) and Panchayat functionaries?
11. Do you find any change in the working of the Panchayat/Gram Sabha now after 1996 Act and before. If so, details?
12. What is the relationship with traditional tribal councils and the Panchayat. Any discord?
13. Are you satisfied with the present arrangements?
14. Do you have any suggestion to improve the working of Panchayat. Please give.

BIBLIOGRAPHY

Books

Heredia, Rudolph C., *Tribal Education for Community Development – A study of Schooling in the Talasari Mission Area,* Concept Publishing Company, New Delhi, 1992.

Scenario of the 7 per cent, Cine mart Foundation, C-619 Safdarjung Development Area, New Delhi, March 1985.

Sharma, B.D., *Planning for Tribals Development,* Prachi Prakasan, New Delhi, 1984.

Status of Panchayati Raj in the States and Union Territories of India, Institute of Social Sciences, Concept Publishing Company, New Delhi, 2000.

Government of India Publications

Administration of Tribal Areas – A Historical Perspective, Xth International Congress of Anthropological and Ethnological Sciences, Ministry of Home Affairs, New Delhi, 1978.

Bhuria Committee Report (Report of Mps And Experts to Make Recommendations on the Salient Features of the Law For Extending Provisions of the Constitution (73rd) Amendment Act 1992 to Scheduled Areas

Provisions in the Constitution of India for Scheduled Tribes, 1978, Ministry of Home Affairs.

Report of the Committee on Special Multi purpose Tribal Blocks, Ministry of Home Affairs, March 1960.

Reports of the Working Group on Welfare and Development of Scheduled Tribes during

(i) Fifth Five Year Plan (1974-79), Ministry of Home Affairs.

(ii) Eighth Five Year Plan, 1990-95, Ministry of Welfare, November 1989.

(iii) Ninth Five Year Plan, 1997-2002, Ministry of Welfare, May 1996

Report of the Scheduled Areas and Scheduled Tribes Commission, Ministry of Home Affairs, 1961.

Scheduled Tribes and Scheduled Areas in India, 1978, Ministry of Home Affairs, New Delhi.

Seventh Plan (1985 –90), Ministry of Welfare

Tribal Development in Fifth Five Year Plan – Some Basic Policy Papers, Vol. I, Ministry of Home Affairs, 1975.

Journals

Monitoring and Evaluation of Tribal Development Programme, The Newsletter, April 1982, Ministry of Home Affairs, New Delhi

Rajiv Gandhi and Panchayati Raj Institutions, Yojana, Vol. 38, No. 13, July 31, 1994

Revamping Panchayati Raj Institutions, Yojana, Vol. 34, Nos. 14 & 15, August 15, 1990.

Role of Panchayati Raj in Shaping the Future of Children by Jon Rohde, Institute of Social Sciences, Occasional Paper 16, 1994.

Tribal Development Policies, Plans and Programmes, Yojana, Vol.44, No. 4 April 2000

INDEX